The Uncensored Home Cook

The Uncensored Home Cook

COMEDIC STORYTELLING OF A
COUNTRY LADY'S RESOLUTION
RECIPES MOST HOME COOKS
ARE TOO AFRAID TO SHARE

• • •

Pearl C. Peebles

ISBN: 1530625564
ISBN 13: 9781530625567

Dedication

• • •

This book is dedicated to my parents, I give God the glory and honor for blessing me with their inheritance. If it was not for their endurance of manual labor, to plant a seed, for their seeds, the breath in my body would have been nonexistent. The foundation that lives within me is because of their sacrifice. The fact that they never gave up, and gave a little more, is the reason I elevate the word "perseverance" to the highest. I am grateful to God for bestowing "favor" on my life. I will forever be indebted to my parents–they are truly missed.

Acknowledgements

• • •

IN MEMORY OF MY *BIG Sister*, your act of kindness and loyalty has left a permanent footprint on this earth. The memory of you saving me a seat on the school bus, to protect me from the school bus bully striking me–still makes me tear up. Your diplomatic way of outsmarting the bully was confirmation–that God always has his angels in place to protect the innocent from being harmed. It was because of your bravery, I was able to return to being a cheery little 1st grader. You were a quiet spirit with a powerful presence. Although, I could never measure up to your greatness, I will continue to be vigilant for standing up for the innocent who have no voice.

To my *Brother and Sister*, thanks for the advice that you have given me over the years. It has been utilized in my journey to finding my purpose. After reading this book, I do hope that my radical sense of humor will not make you disown me. If shame should come upon you, please find a paper bag to conceal your identity;

To the *Nieces, Great Nieces, Nephews, and Great Nephews*, there's too many of you, to acknowledge each of you. With that said, "Stay out of trouble, and go to bed!";

To *Cousin Bea*, thanks for working hard to feed your four children and me. For some reason, I always knew when supper time was being served at your house;

To *Uncle Vandy and Aunt Princess*, thanks for always showing up–your presence in my life will never be forgotten;

To *The Ellingtons*, thanks for your longstanding friendship;

To *Dr. Gwen*, thanks for being the *"Finalization Taste Officer (FTO)"* for this comedic cookbook; your constructive feedback was truly valued;

To *Dr. Teresa*, thanks for your ministry and guidance–you are confirmation that sisterhood still exist;

To *Janet B.*, thanks for laughing with me until tear drops were formed–it gave me the courage to pursue a career in making others laugh as well;

To *Izzy*, thanks for coping with my talkative episodes for so long. Tell *Mr. P.*, I'm doing less talking, and more writing these days;

To *Harry W.*, thanks for bringing the "visual" to my 1st authored comedic cookbook.

Cooking Advisory Statement

• • •

In life, every foot that touches this great earth has a purpose for being present. Some of us know early on, while some of us find their purpose just in the nick of time. Whenever you find your true purpose, it's better to find it, than to leave this world without ever acting on it.

As you begin to read this comedic cookbook, you will recognize a "Cooking Advisory Tip (CAT)" throughout. Please, don't be startled with some of my outlandish cooking tips or advice. I want you to know, I did not compromise the taste of these recipes to get you to laugh. It's just that, I had to release some of these conversations in my head–before another family member was admitted to the hospital from exhaustion. I hope you are sympathetic to my comedic storytelling, it was written for the reader who was hungry, and too proud to laugh.

Every Day You Wake Up

• • •

EVERY DAY YOU WAKE UP is an opportunity to be better and do better.

If a person presents themselves to you, as not having means for food, show them kindness for their lawful act of asking you, versus an unlawful act of taking it from you.

If you have slandered someone's good name, be the bigger person, and own up to what you have done, by recanting your statement to the audience that heard it first.

If you have taken advantage of someone who was there to ease strife in your life, show them their sacrifice and kindness was not taken for granted, by succeeding in the goal that was originally set-forth.

If you are a person with a conscious, you will always sleep peacefully and soundly.

Every day you wake up, should not be wasted, allow your presence to be an example of faith, hope, and perseverance.

Table of Contents

Toothless Meals: Soft to the teeth recipes for persons who have been "gumming it" for too long.

• • •

Easy on the Gums Beef Stew

If your dentist has informed you it will take several months to customize a pair of dentures for your mouth, due your insistence on preparing "hard as a brick" meals, this simply means, your teeth are damage, and you will be "gumming it" for awhile. Remain calm, take a deep breath, and try not to have thoughts of your dentist becoming wealthy from this extensive dental work. Right now, you have more critical issues to focus on—like how to cook moist foods for your sensitive gums. Don't fret, there is a resolution recipe for you, if you are willing to accept advice from an "Uncensored Home Cook" who needs some book sales. Right now, you must do whatever it takes to prevent yourself from starving. All you have to do is, dig deep within your cabinets, reach out, grab it, and embrace it. See how simple that was–now you can get to cooking some of this beef stew in that crockpot!

For every resolution recipe, there is a lesson to be learned even it does not make sense to the reader. That lesson for this storyline is, "An underutilized appliance will bring relief to your gums, if you are willing to wipe the dust off it!"

Ingredients

3 pound of beef chuck or stew meat (cut into 1-inch cubes)
3 whole carrots (sliced)
1 packet beefy onion soup & dip mix (follow package directions)
4 cups water
2 (14.5 oz.) can butter beans
1 (14.5 oz.) can diced tomato w/garlic

4 thyme sprigs (fresh)
1 medium onion (chopped)
1 garlic clove
½ tsp. allspice
1 tsp. cumin
1 tsp. seasoning salt
½ tsp. black pepper
1 tsp. Worcestershire sauce

Step 1: Season beef with seasoning salt and marinate in refrigerator overnight. Prior to placing beef in crockpot, bring to room temperature for 1 hour.

Step 2: In the crockpot, add beef soup packet and water. Add seasoned beef, carrots, tomato, thyme, onion, garlic, allspice, cumin, black pepper, and Worcestershire sauce. Cover and cook for 6 hours.

Step 3: Add 1 can of the butter beans 1 to 2 hours prior to the end of cooking time. At the same time, dump the remaining can of butter beans in a mixing bowl and ladle 1 cup of broth from crockpot. Use a blender or Immersion Hand Blender to puree beans. Pour puree beans back into crockpot (puree will thicken your soup) and continue cooking the allotted time. Make 8 to 10 servings.

Cooking Advisory Tip: Before indulging in this delicious beef stew, allow it to cool to eliminate the risk of any burns to the gums. The objective of this stew is to be easy on the gums, not blistering the gums.

Almost Momma's Chicken and Dumplings

If your family consists of five or more people, you might want to consider preparing a one pot meal–it's a "stress free" way of cooking. For my mother, chicken and dumplings was the one pot meal that kept her family silent. Once you have adapted to this method of cooking, you will become more sympathetic to:

* Scraping the bottom of the pot to obtain the last bit of food crumbs for the neighbor's greedy kid, who conveniently makes nightly visits to your house for dinner–you might want to consider anonymously adopting the kid for a tax exemption;
* Returning your neighbor's Dutch oven pot that you conveniently borrowed six months ago, for a "make believe" dinner party; and
* Giving your spouse an overdue "fatback grease" massage under a 1977 mirrored disco ball.

However, you choose to conduct your post cooking escapades, is strictly your business. At the end of day, all that matter is, you have finally created a delicious dumpling–that will stick to your families' teeth.

Ingredients

2 cups shredded rotisserie chicken
1 (32 oz.) box chicken broth
2 (10 ¾ oz.) cans cream chicken soup
½ cup onions

¼ cup fresh carrots
¼ cup tiny peas (frozen)
1 tsp. thyme
½ tsp. black pepper
2 tbsps. margarine

Dumpling

1 cup herb seasoned classic stuffing
1/3 cup self-rising flour
1/3 cup light cream or milk
1 tsp. black pepper
1 egg (beaten)

Step 1: In a heated Dutch oven pot, melt margarine; add onions, carrots, peas, black pepper, and thyme. Sauté for 3 minutes or until vegetables are translucent.

Step 2: Add rotisserie chicken, chicken broth, and cream of chicken soup to pot. Cook uncovered for about 30 minutes or until thicken.

Step 3: In a mixing bowl, whisk the egg and add cream, stuffing, flour, and black pepper. Don't over mix the batter; it should be a "thick" consistency with a minimum amount of liquid.

Step 4: Using the 2 spoons method, scoop dumpling batter with 1 spoon and use the other spoon to release dumpling batter into soup. Cover pot and cook dumplings for approximately 10 minutes or until firm. Remove pot from heat and enjoy. Make 4 servings.

Cooking Advisory Tip: As you make this recipe, you will realize the salt was omitted. If you prefer to add salt to this recipe, because you are trying to prove to your boss, you really do have hypertension from job stress, please do it at your own discretion. I will not be offended or envious of you–for receiving six months of "shady medical leave."

Momma's Rehab Pinto Bean Soup

Whenever hard times had come to my family due to low tobacco revenue, there was a strong reliance of pinto beans for our meals. I recall my mother preparing a repeated meal of pinto beans and corn bread to eliminate our stomachs from waking her up at night. Although the meals were very delicious, I couldn't help expressing my concerns to my mother regarding our daily consumption of pinto beans. The dismay on my mother's face made me realize, I should always show gratitude for the hands that prepares my food–and I should have forewarn my teacher, in advance, to place my desk in the back of the classroom–during times pinto beans were being consumed at my house.

In honor of such wonderful and loving Mother, this recipe is for you. Hope you are laughing in the big sky.

Ingredients

   1 (20 oz.) pkg. pinto beans
   1 cup chunky salsa (medium, hot or mild)
   1 smoke turkey wing or leg
   1 package smoke kielbasa sausage (sliced)
   3 ½ cups water
   1 tbsp. cumin
   ½ tsp. salt
   ½ tsp. black pepper
   3 garlic cloves
   1 medium onion

Overnight: Soak beans overnight or 6 to 8 hours before cooking. Drain water in colander, rinse and pick through beans to remove debris.

Cooking: Set crockpot on "high" temperature. Add beans, water, salsa, turkey, cumin, onions, and garlic. Cook for 6 hours. Within 5 hours of cooking, remove turkey from crockpot and pulled turkey meat off bone and set aside.

Ladle 3 cups of beans from crockpot and puree in a blender. Pour puree beans back into the crockpot. Add the pulled turkey meat, kielbasa sausage, salt, and pepper. Cook for an additional 35 minutes to ensure the smoke flavor of kielbasa is released. Serve solo or over rice. Make 6 to 8 servings.

Cooking Advisory Tip: If you are a first time bean cooker, I would suggest that you follow the soaking instruction. This will allow suffi- cient time for the "gases" to be released from these beans. If you chose not to follow this CAT tip, and want to cook this recipe your way, please proceed with caution when attending gatherings in small venues and long road trips in vanpools–you can't say I did not forewarn you!

BLACKEN FISH

If you have never blackened fish, one would think it means to burn it up. In actuality, you are burning the fish up, but with added flavor. Basically, you're just massaging black pepper, or other dry seasonings into a fish to be seared in a screaming hot pan. Once the fish is seared, the coloration will began to look like sand with black pepper incorporated in it. This simply means, the fish is perfectly cooked. Now, if there's no visibility of the fish during the blackening process, there's a probability your house is on fire–and you need to get the hell out of there!

What should we all take away from this story? Just because you can burn in the kitchen, does not give you the right to burn down the kitchen!

INGREDIENTS

> 4 pieces tilapia or cod fish
> 2 ½ tbsps. garlic herb seasoning blend (no salt)
> 1 tsp. black pepper
> 1 lemon
> 3 tbsps. oil

Preheat a large skillet with oil.

In a mixing bowl, mix together the black pepper and garlic herb seasoning. Massage seasoning over each fish. Place fish in "hot" pan and cook 2 minutes on each side. Remove from pan unto a plate–squeeze lemon juice for added flavor. Make 4 servings.

Cooking Advisory Tip: If you do not have any intentions of burning down a house, this would be a good recipe for burning off those unwanted pounds.

Cauliflower & Shrimp Medallions

When I brainstorm for a resolution recipe creation, my objective is to tailor the recipe to a problematic situation. Sometimes it could be a recipe to reunite a "hate you but love" relationship, or a specialty meal to get them out the house for good. No matter what the issue is, there should be a recipe that is connected to your specific issue. For example, for this "Cauliflower & Shrimp Medallions" recipe, I wanted it to be eatable, tasty, and delicate. More specifically, it was for the person with sensitive teeth, and person(s) who did not want to wear their teeth. In my kitchen, there is always a recipe to resolve or improve a problematic situation.

Ingredients

> 1 whole cauliflower (chopped to florets)
> 1 ½ cup deveined shrimp (diced)
> 2 egg whites
> 2 tbsps. butter
> ½ tsp. onion salt
> ½ tsp. black pepper
> 4 cups water

Step 1: In a medium sauce pan, add water and bring to boil. Add cauliflower and cook for approximately 15 minutes. Once cauliflower is cooked, drain water and transfer to a medium bowl. Mash cauliflower with a potato masher. Add onion salt and pepper, and set aside to cool for 20 minutes.

Step 2: In a medium size pan, sauté shrimp with butter for approximately 8 minutes. Remove from pan and set aside on paper towel.

Step 3: In a mixing bowl, add mash cauliflower, egg whites, and shrimp. Mix until ingredients are incorporated.

Step 4: On a sheet pan, spray the pan with non-stick spray. Place an egg mold on sheet pan and take a handful of cauliflower mixture from the bowl, and press into the mold–release mold once patty is formed. Repeat process until there are 6 medallions. Place pan under the broiler under "high" temperature for 20 minutes or until patties are firm. Remove from broiler and cool. Garnish with sauce recipe below. Make 6 servings.

SAUCE

¼ cup dice tomatoes
¼ cup light cream
½ tsp. Old Bay seasoning
½ tsp. sugar

In a small sauce pan, add tomatoes, Old Bay, light cream, and sugar. Cook mixture for 12 minutes or until sauce thickens. Pour sauce over medallions and enjoy a light way of indulging.

Cooking Advisory Tip: If your stomach is "growling" for a different kind of protein for this recipe, you can always incorporate chicken, ham, spam, tuna, or cooked sausage into the cauliflower mash mixture.

Almost Minestrone Soup

Don't you just hate it, when you are preparing a traditional recipe and you don't have all the required ingredients? I'm sure this dilemma has happened to many Home Cooks who were trying to follow a celebrity chef who made it look effortless. Well, if you are from the "Make Do Generation (MDG)," like me, you will be able to improvise with whatever food that is strategically placed in your cupboard.

Upon entering your "sanctuary of fulfillment," please analyze your options before grabbing your ingredients–you don't want to mistakenly take a can of Buster's dog food for a can of tomatoes. I'm sure Buster will not appreciate this selfish act of yours. Just stay the course, and get in and out of that cupboard. Your objective is to properly execute the recipe so you can feed your adult children another free meal. I'm sure they will embrace your efforts with open "cash free" hands.

At the end of the day, I hope this recipe will encourage you to take a risk, in rehabbing a traditional recipe that could possibly taste better than the original one.

Ingredients

2 (28 oz.) cans crush tomatoes (w/basil, garlic, & oregano)
1 (12 oz.) pkg. green beans (frozen)
1 (16 oz.) pkg. baby lima beans (frozen)
1 (10 oz.) pkg. chopped spinach (frozen)
1 (32 oz.) box vegetable stock
1/3 cup light cream
4 tbsps. agave

1 cup onion
1 tbsp. salt
1 tbsp. black pepper
4 tbsps. olive oil or vegetable oil

Preheat a large pot or Dutch oven with oil. Add onions, salt, and black pepper, sauté until translucent. Add tomatoes, vegetable stock, and cream. Boil for 5 minutes, and add green/lima beans, spinach, and agave. Cook on medium heat for 15 minutes. Cover and simmer soup for an additional 35 minutes. Ladle the soup into bowls and garnish with shredded parmesan cheese and serve. Make 6 to 8 servings.

Cooking Advisory Tip: This is a good soup to keep stocked in the freezer for those "pop up" relatives who just happen to roll up in your camp unannounced. Bowl it up for them, and go to bed like they are not even there–maybe next time they will call in advance to avoid eating in the dark.

Soul Poetry Chowder

In the early '70s, it was not unusual for men to utilize a little of "Soul Poetry (SP)" to obtain the women of their dreams. It was the "Can you dig it?," poetry sited from the soul. Phrases like, "Um.....Um.....Um.....you so fine, I'm going to stay home from work just to absorb all that fineness!" That was the type of rap that would win a woman's heart and give her a good chuckle at the same time. Even if the brother was broke, and could not make the women his life partner, it was his SP that made him stand out from the stuck up brother. This was the era that inspired me to use comedy as a way to communicate with others.

Since this a comedic cookbook, it would only be fitting that I put down some of my own SP, in memory of those forgotten poetic soul rapper, this one is for you: "You are the CINNAMON in my butter, the CAYENNE in my fire, and the HAM in my YAMS!" That's what you call "Soul Poetry Chowder," can you chowder that?

Ingredients

> 3 medium sweet potatoes (diced)
> 2 cups boneless ham steak (diced)
> 1 ½ cups low sodium chicken stock
> ½ (8oz.) cinnamon cream cheese (room temperature)
> 2 tbsps. unsalted butter or margarine
> 1 cup light cream
> 5 cups water
> ¼ tsp. cinnamon
> ¼ tsp. nutmeg
> ¼ tsp. cayenne pepper
> ¼ cup onions

In medium sauce pan, bring water and potatoes to boil. Once potatoes are fork tender, drain and set aside.

In a large pot or Dutch oven, heat butter or margarine; add onions, ham, cayenne pepper, nutmeg, and cinnamon, cook for 8 minutes. Stir in the cream cheese until melted and add cream, chicken stock, and potatoes. Cook uncovered for 20 minutes. Ladle soup in bowls and bring the season of fall into your home. Make 4 servings.

Cooking Advisory Tip: Have a candle light dinner for two, and put back the SWEET in your sweet potatoes.

CHAPTER 2

High Risk Recipes: Dangerously delicious
meals that will give you the courage to cook
and reduce further criminal activity.

• • •

BUCKET LIST BELL PEPPER SOUP

Eventually, all of us will become elderly if we live long enough. When that time finally arrives, we should embrace it with joy and gratitude. That simply means, "Elderly people have paid their dues to society, and don't bring them any drama–they will always outsmart you, or knock some common sense into you."

I want to paint a picture of a situation that could possible cause harm to you if you are not "coming correct" with an elderly person. Let's say, you have an elderly neighbor who is pleading with you to call the authorities on this bank teller who has been pocketing senior citizens' money during cash withdrawals at the bank. As her neighbor, you have to do the right thing and turn in your wife. It is to your advantage to take these allegations seriously. You should be grateful your elderly neighbor is giving you more than enough time to get your finances together prior to becoming a single parent. Don't make it harder on yourself by reminiscing about the lavish lifestyle that your wife provided for the family. Hopefully, the police will discretely take care of this matter, right after they finish devouring their daily meal–at your elderly neighbor's house.

What's the lesson learned from this story, "A delicious homecook meal will give you all the power and protection needed to fight criminal activity."

INGREDIENTS

2 lbs. ground chicken
3 green bell peppers (finely diced)

1 (32 oz.) box vegetable stock
2 tbsps. ketchup
1 large onion (finely diced)
1 tbsp. minced garlic
1 cup water
1 tbsp. cumin
1 tsp. salt
1 tsp. black pepper
4 tbsps. canola oil

Step 1: In a large pot or Dutch oven, heat canola oil. Add peppers, onions, and garlic; sauté for 3 minutes or until veggies are translucent. Add ground chicken, cumin, salt, and black pepper and cook for approximately 2 minutes.

Step 2: Stir in ketchup, stock, and water. Bring to a boil and simmer on medium heat for 30 minutes. Ladle up in a bowl and enjoy. Make 4 to 6 servings.

Cooking Advisory Tip: This is a quick soup for the elderly person who still enjoys cooking. Keep moving, we really need your wisdom, and some delicious homecooked meals.

Itchy Good Crab Cakes

Living in the great State of Maryland, I had the pleasure of enjoying some of the meatiest crab cakes. They were sometimes too enormous for one person to consume in one sitting. Unfortunately, due to allergic reactions of seafood, some of us will never have the opportunity to enjoy the deliciousness of a crab cake. If you are one of those people who really enjoys a crab cake, but have been lying to cover up your real itch problem, than you might want to:

1. Contact an unauthorized "Country Folks 991 Operator" to find out, if Doctor Root has any plans to come out of retirement to fix that problematic itch of yours;
2. Have an impromptu family meeting if the itching has spread from the neck to the lower roots–there's a pretty good chance the court will be serving you divorce papers within 24 hours; and
3. Refrain from patting the rescue dog that was recently taken into your home. He is tired of your unclean hands on him, and you using his infestation problem as an excuse for your scratching episodes.

If none of these issues are applicable to you, please proceed in making these delicious crab cakes.

Ingredients

1 pound jumbo crab meat (pick for shells)
15 saltine crackers (finely crushed)
½ cup mayonnaise

4 eggs whites (reserve 1 for egg white for egg wash)
1 tablespoon Dijon mustard
1 tbsp. of Worcestershire sauce
½ tsp. hot sauce
1 tbsp. red bell pepper (finely diced)
1 tsp. of parsley
½ lemon wedge
Nonstick spray

Preheat oven broiler on high.

Step 1: Drain liquid off crab meat. In a large bowl, dump crab meat and gently pull apart with hands to remove shells. Add crackers, red bell pepper, and parsley. Set aside.

Step 2: In a small mixing bowl, whisk mayonnaise, eggs, mustard, Worcestershire sauce, and hot sauce. Pour mixture over crab ingredients. Gently use your hands to mix all ingredients together. Form 3 inch crab cakes and refrigerate for 1 hour or overnight for firmness.

Step 3: Spray sheet pan with nonstick spray and place no more than 3 crab cakes on sheet pan. Brush each crab cake with egg wash (mix 1 tsp. of water and egg white). Place crab cakes in broiler for 10 to 12 minutes. Monitor cakes until you have the desired brownness. Remove crab cakes from oven and cool for 5 minutes. Transfer to plate and squeeze lemon juice for added flavor. Make 6 patties.

Cooking Advisory Tip: If you have not developed an "itch" problem from eating these crab cakes, than you might want to make a smaller version of the crab cakes into some "Party Teasers" (appetizers).

Speedy Cabbage

If you were once a teenager and now a parent, you can expect to receive an enormous amount of "karma" from your offspring–just the way you packaged it up to your parent(s). Be prepared to have sleepless nights and impromptu outbursts on anyone who seems to be vulnerable. Forget you are a parent, it does not matter anymore–because your offspring will be regulating your household as if they are paying the bills up in that camp. Don't ignore it–you need a strategy to keep you occupied until you find a solution. Take this time to prepare this "Speedy Cabbage" so you will have a little more time to:

1. Plot on how to get the family fed without anyone noticing there is one family member missing from the table; and
2. Use the cabbage diet as an "alibi" to distract suspicious parties from discovery the real reason you lost 15 pounds.

Regardless how you implement these steps, I do hope that you will take the time out of your busy schedule, to fuel up with one of the easiest vegetable to prepare–for whenever stressful situations should come your way.

Ingredients

1 medium cabbage (chopped)
1 large white onion (diced)
3 garlic cloves
2 tbsps. margarine
1 tsp. salt
1 tsp black pepper
1 tsp. garlic powder
¼ cup water

In a large pot, add margarine. Once margarine has melted, add onions, garlic, salt, pepper, and garlic powder. Sauté over medium heat for 5 minutes and fold in cabbage and add water. Thoroughly stir all ingredients and simmer for an additional 15 minutes and serve as prepared. Make 4 to 6 servings.

Cooking Advisory Tip: If there are too many "dramatic episodes" going on at your house, you might want to consider enrolling the offspring in some "acting" classes–to release some of that bottled up tension.

Banger Resolution Drumsticks

For those parent(s) who have a young adult that is affiliated with an "Unrecognizable Organization (UO)," you must be going through it. This organization is causing havoc in your household because they have gone unrecognized by the local authorities. If you want to cut down on your young adult's quality time with an UO, make sure you are incorporating a "high risk" vegetable in their diet. This will not only do the trick, it will give them a much needed reality check.

In order for this recipe to work in your favor, you will have to be patient during this experimental time period. Once your young adult has devoured these "spicy" drumsticks, the after effects will require extensive healing from the hidden habanero peppers. Try not to show any emotions of happiness as the young adult looks to you for a resolution. Hopefully, by the time this healing process has played itself out, you will have gotten back some overdue respect, a good night sleep, and a transformation of an unruly young adult who now lives for humanitarian causes. Who says you can't reduce potential criminal activity with the right recipe.

Ingredients

> 8 drumsticks (w/skin)
> 2 cups herb stuffing
> 2 baked potatoes (pre-cooked)
> 2 habanero chili peppers finely chopped (optional)
> 1 red bell pepper
> 8 tbsps. butter or margarine (softened)
> 2 tbsps. vegetable
> 1 tsp. salt
> 1 tsp. black pepper

Preheat oven to 400° degrees.

Step 1: In a medium bowl, mash potatoes with butter. Add herb stuffing, chili peppers, bell pepper, and salt. Mix all ingredients with hand and set aside.

Step 2: Pat drumsticks dry with a paper towel. With your fingers between the skins, slowly pull skin away from flesh of chicken to create a pocket. Take a handful of stuffing mixture and stuff underneath skin of drumstick. Use a piece of twine to wrap around the opened area to ensure stuffing is secured. Repeat process until all of the drumsticks are stuffed.

Step 3: Rub butter or margarine on flesh of drumsticks. Sprinkle stuff drumsticks with black pepper. Place drumsticks on a sheet pan with a rack, bake for 40 minutes. Remove from oven and cover with foil for 10 minutes to allow juices to redistribute. Make 8 servings.

Cooking Advisory Tip: If you do decide to add the habanero chili peppers, please DO NOT give it to seniors, small children, and pets. The habanero chili pepper should only be utilized on "healthy" misbehaving individuals who need to stay in the house!

OUT OF THYME CONFECTIONARY CHICKEN

Back in the day, a number of our country relatives who were exhausted from working on the farm, eventually migrated up North to apply their farming skills into new business ventures. Gossip at the country Shot Houses (SH) revealed that the City Relatives (CR) had opened bakery shops within their communities to support Home Cooks who were interested in distributing "altered" produce. It sure was good to hear those CRs had continued to use their farming skills for the better good.

From the caring country kin folks' perspective, the CRs solidified the true meaning of success with their fancy cars, fashionable clothes, and bedazzling gold jewelry. With this type of status, the country kin folks felt the CRs good deeds should not go unnoticed. Therefore, a call was placed to city officials to convince them to honor the CRs with a special recognition award for all of their philanthropy work within the community. Within 24 hours, officials arrived unannounced to chauffeur the CRs to a "spiffy" banquet hall. They were all given the royal treatment along with an "Out of Thyme" award for being extremely modest for producing some of the best heart racing produce throughout the community.

Although it took some time, the CRs' business ventures were finally accepted into the law books. If there is anything to learn from a CRs transformation of produce, it would have to be, "Never run away from doing your chores, because eventually you will have to complete them in a facility with folks who are not even kin to you!"

INGREDIENTS

10 chicken tenderloins
1 cup buttermilk
1 cup confectionary sugar
1½ cup flour
¼ cup thyme

Preheat oven for 400° degrees.

Step 1: In a medium bowl, mix buttermilk and sugar. Place chicken into mixture and refrigerate for 1 hour or overnight. Remove from refrigerator; allow chicken to rest 1 hour at room temperature.

Step 2: In 2 separate mixing bowls, add flour and thyme. Dread the chicken in flour and then thyme. Repeat steps until all the chicken tenderloins have been dread. Place chicken on sheet pan with rack and cook for 40 to 45 minutes. Remove from oven and cool. Make 6 to 8 servings.

Cooking Advisory Tip: Don't allow thyme to run out on you, create a "legitimate" vegetable garden in your community.

Cereal Killer Cupcakes

Before there is criticism of this title, be mindful, that this is a "high risk" recipe creation. If you are too afraid to follow the storyline for this recipe, in fear of discovering the truth about your mate, I won't hold it against you.

This recipe was inspired by this fine looking car salesman who couldn't convince me to buy a new car while my car was receiving an oil change. To describe him, let's just say, "He was the "make believe" man that I could finally introduce to my family and friends." This brother had a "fresh" clean detergent smell, baking soda white teeth, and pliable fatback grease skin. Yes, these were all the attributes a Country Lady, like myself, had wanted in a man.

After a one dinner invite, and a rough handling my dog to rollover, I never saw Mr. Fine again–until his face was splattered on the 10:00 o'clock News for impersonating a law enforcement official. Apparently, he befriended this lady so he could gain access into her apartment to pursue his part-time job of criminal activity. Who would have believed that Mr. Fine was working two jobs–I guess you'll never know what a person will do just to make ends meet.

I hope this this story will inspire you to observe your mate's behavior a little deeper. If you are not certain if your mate or potential mate is everything you dream of–or the person who will make sure you never wake up from a dream, maybe the following hypotheticals will convince you otherwise:

1. He arrives home sweaty and exhausted prior to the 11:00 o'clock News being aired, and he does not have a gym membership–there's strong possibility of criminal activity;

2. When you don't purchase his favorite cereal from the grocery store, he becomes enraged and leaves town for a couple of days–there's a strong possibility your mortgage payment will be late again; and

3. Your dog no longer greets him at the door–this is an indicator your dog has fled to the local dog shelter because they are the only ones that can give him immunity.

If none of these occurrences are happening in your household, be thankful that your mate has switch from cold cereal to hot oatmeal.

INGREDIENTS

1 cup all-purpose flour (sifted)
4 cups whole cinnamon toasted cereal (Yields 2 cups after pulsed in Food Processor–reserve ½ cup for topping)
½ cup whole oats (pulse in Food Processor)
1 cup granulated sugar
1 ¼ tsp. baking powder
1 ¼ tsp. baking soda
1 tsp. salt
1 cup whole milk
2 large eggs (room temperature)
3 tsps. banana extract
¼ cup vegetable oil
¼ cup boiling water

Preheat oven to 350° degrees.

Step 1: In a Food Processor, add cinnamon toast cereal and oats, pulse until it is finely grind into a flour mixture. Transfer cereal mixture to a large mixing bowl. Sift in the flour and then add sugar, salt, baking soda, and baking powder. Mix dry ingredients together and set aside.

Step 2: In small bowl, beat eggs and transfer to dry ingredients. Add milk, oil, and banana extract. Beat all ingredients with hand mixer on medium speed for 1 minute. Add boiling water and beat batter for 1 minute until combined.

Step 3: Pour batter from mixing bowl into a measuring cup (the batter is easier to pour into cupcake cups). Line the cupcake pan with cupcake cups. Pour ½ of batter into each cup. After all cups have been filled, top each cupcake with the reserve cinnamon toasted cereal. Place in oven and cook for 18 to 20 minutes or until the toothpick comes out clean from the "toothpick test." Remove cupcakes from oven and cool for 10 minutes. Makes 22 to 24 cupcakes.

Cooking Advisory Tip: If you have made these cupcakes and they were executed with deliciousness, you have succeeded with "freeing up" your mate's hands from further criminal activity.

SPICY PINEAPPLE ORANGE CHICKEN

As you go through life changes, everybody has a "spicy" past that they would like to confide in someone. Whether it's a clergy, bartender, relative, neighbor, or your dog, everybody is seeking out someone to share their darkest secrets with. Sometimes that person could arrive at the least likely places. That would be the case of an after work "Happy Hour" with my friends on Halloween eve. At the round table where we sat, my friends and I were the only patrons occupying the table until a "jittery" looking man pulled his chair next to mines. Due to fact, that I believe a man should run after me, I allowed him to initiate the conversation. Eventually, he spoke the four words that no single, vulnerable Country Lady, living in metropolitan city, wanted to hear:

Jittery Man
"I just got out!"

Country Lady
"Oh, you just got out for the evening?"

Jittery Man
"I just got out!"

Country Lady
Oh………you just got out! I see, "What were you in for?"
(My nightlight finally flicked on.)

Jittery Man
Attempted murder!
(Said it with conviction)

Country Lady
For real, you don't say.
(Logical reply if you did not have anywhere to run to.)

Jittery Man
They said I was trying to kill my girlfriend–but she lied to
the police.
(He proceeded to sweat, as he relived the events that led to
his imprisonment.)

Country Lady
Is she still alive?

Jittery Man
Yeah!
(His reply triggered anger.)

Country Lady
Well, I don't see how they could call it "attempted murder"
if she's still alive.
(Had to gain his trust–in case he had plans on carrying out
an "actual" murder.)

Jittery Man
You're right.
(He seemed relieved that he had confessed his sins to a
wholesome looking Country Lady.)

Country Lady
Well, it was nice talking to you, have a bless evening.

(After 30 minutes of his testimony, and not being able to render a verdict, he spotted another "potential" victim signaling him to come over–they danced the evening away.)

Although I was exhausted from the spicy information that I had obtained, I realized, "If you want to receive a monetary reward from a "Cold Case" mystery, you should welcome a conversation with a jittery and sweaty man–who does not have time to wipe the sweat off his face."

Preheat oven to 400° degrees.

INGREDIENTS

10 party wings
2 tbsp. sweet orange marmalade
1 tbsp. fresh ginger (grated)
1 cup crushed pineapples w/juice
½ habanero chili pepper (whole one for extra spiciness)
2 tbsp. agave nectar
¼ tsp. garlic powder
¼ tsp. salt
4 tbsp. unsalted butter
½ lime

Step 1: In a medium mixing bowl, add chicken and sprinkle with garlic powder and salt. Place wings in oven and bake for 40 minutes. Remove from oven and set aside.

Step 2: In large sauce pan, sauté the chili pepper in butter. Grate in ginger and add pineapples, marmalade, and agave. Squeeze the lime juice over mixture. Cook mixture for 15 minutes or until sauce thickens.

Step 3: Transfer wings to pineapple orange sauce and toss until coated. Remove wings from heat, and serve over sautéed cabbage. Make 4 servings.

Cooking Advisory Tip: Try this recipe at your next party—it might just open up your guest to confess their darkest secrets.

Witness Protection Program (WPP) Meat Sauce

Law enforcement, "Do you have a witness that was forced to enter your "Witness Protection Program (WPP)?" Do you feel they will be fleeing from the Safe House (SH) before giving their sweaty testimony? Well, don't worry anymore, because I have just the recipe that will confine them to any undisclosed location. Try my "WPP Meat Sauce," within an hour of eating a generous amount of servings, your witness will fall down on their knees for another plea deal. The grease in itself will clog their arteries just enough to stop them from running a full block. Hopefully, for them, this experience will be a good life lesson of what really happens when you don't pour the leftover grease into a grease can.

Ingredients

3 pounds ground beef
3 pounds ground pork
2 pounds of sausage
2 cups leftover can grease (key ingredient)
2¼ cup heavy cream
6 garlic cloves
1 large onion
2 bay leaves
3 tbsps. salt

Preheat a large skillet.

In medium pan, pour leftover grease and heat until melted. Add garlic, onions, ground beef, pork, sausage, and heavy cream.

Cook ingredients until fully cooked. Transfer to a measuring cup "WITHOUT" draining off the grease. This process will allow the authorities to monitor the amount of meat sauce the witness is devouring.

HILARIOUS WARNING: THERE IS NO SERVING SIZE FOR THIS CONCOCTION.

Cooking Advisory Tip: If you are in the WPP program, the Department's physician should monitor the witness' cholesterol levels during the time period this meat sauce has been devoured. If you have concerns this recipe is too much of a "high risk," may I suggest a friendly version of my "Fully Dressed Chili" following this recipe. See, what a nice Country Lady I am, I thought ahead by creating a meat sauce recipe that is not detrimental to your arteries.

Fully Dressed Chili

The one thing I can't stand is going to a cookout and there's no chili prepared for the hotdogs. If there was a term called "Food Pet Peeve (FPP)," this would be a FPP. Who forgets to prepare homemade chili to pour over hotdogs before a cookout? If you are not leaving the house undressed, "Why would you want to see an undressed hotdog?" I know I can't be the only person that's feeling this way, there has to be some freeloading people out there, who are too ashamed to speak up. Maybe they will come forth after reading this short story.

For me, my first encounter with a fully dressed hotdog was at the age of four, when my mother placed an order at the local diner for two hotdogs with chili, raw onions, relish, and mustard. You would have thought my mother would have consulted with me prior to placing the order, to confirm whether or not I would eat all those unusual toppings on my hotdog. I guess a Mother knows her child, and my mother knew that I was the greediest child that she had. When the hotdog arrived for me to restrain it with my tiny hands, I tore it up, and had the nerve to ask my mother for another one. It was at that moment, I vowed, that when I became an adult, and could afford to feed my penny pinching relatives, I would make sure that every hotdog would always be fully dressed.

Now that you know my personal story of a fully dressed hotdog, I hope you will find it in your heart, to contribute more money to your next family cookout, to decrease your chances of being called a "name" you don't want to own up to.

Ingredients

1 pound lean ground meat (80% lean 20% fat)
1 (14.5 oz.) can dice tomatoes

2 garlic cloves
½ medium onions
¼ tsp. garlic powder
¼ tsp. chili powder
¼ tsp. cumin
¼ tsp. salt
1 tbsp. canola oil

Preheat skillet with oil.

Step 1: In a mixing bowl, season the meat with garlic powder, chili powder, cumin, and salt.

Step 2: To the skillet, add garlic and onions, sauté for 1 minute. Add seasoned meat to the pan and cook for 10 minutes or until fully cooked. Transfer cooked meat to plate lined with paper towel to drain off grease. Wipe pan with a paper towel or clean cloth. Transfer meat back to the pan and add tomatoes. Simmer sauce for 20 minutes and remove from heat and serve. Make 4 to 6 servings.

Cooking Advisory Tip: If you are attending a cookout, cook the chili the day prior to the gathering–it will give the seasonings an opportunity to marry each other for extra goodness.

School Bus Mackerel Fish Cakes

Parent(s), if you want to ensure your offspring will leave your house at age 18 and get their Omega 3 when departing, than you will need to keep plenty cans of mackerel fish in your pantry. I know this could be a "high risk" situation for your precious little offspring, but it's for their own good. From grade school to high school, my mother would regularly prepare mackerel fish cakes for our breakfast before we board the school bus. I had no complaints whatsoever because it was some good eating. Personally, if it was not for those mackerel fish cakes, I would not be the person I am today.

To be more specific, on how mackerel fish impacted my life, I would say, it was the leftover juice on my cheek. It gave me the confidence and resilience to get on that school bus and hold my head up high. Now, I will admit, there was teasing from the school bus bully, but I didn't allow him to rattle me when it came to eating my mother's mackerel fish cakes. He was probably resentful because I did not bring him one to enjoy. I sure wish I had given him one–maybe the fish smell would have gotten him thrown off the bus for good.

I'm telling you, if you want to test your child's ability to deal with strife, "School Bus Mackerel Fish Cakes," will either make them stand up for your honor, or get them out of your house to start a new life–where no one will ever know their nickname was "Mackerel."

INGREDIENTS

1 (14.75 oz.) can mackerel fish
12 whole wheat saltine crackers (finely crushed)
½ onions
¼ cup red peppers
1 egg
¼ tsp. smoky paprika
1 tsp. of salt
1 tsp. of black pepper
4 tbsps. canola oil

Preheat skillet with oil.

Step 1: Remove fish from can and dump in a large bowl. Remove bone and skin and disregard. Add crackers, onions, peppers, paprika, salt, black pepper, and egg. Mix ingredients with hands and form a patty. Place in refrigerator for 30 minutes or overnight to firm up.

Step 2: Place 3 patties in skillet and cook until crisp on each side. Remove fish from pan and drain on paper towel. Serve solo or on a toasted bun. Make 6 patties.

Cooking Advisory Tip: If your child decides to do their homework assignment while eating these mackerel fish cakes, please ensure there is plenty of "fish juice" on their homework paper. This act of kindness will ensure the teacher will automatically pass your child to the next grade–just to get that "fishy" smell out of her classroom!

A Ruthless Meatball Head

If your supervisor has instructed only you to evacuate the building during a hostile protesters' rally, "Would you follow his order?" Well, if he could not confirm if the protestors personally invited you to attend the rally, may I suggest, "That you remain in your ripped up office chair." If your colleagues are not moving their feet, this should be confirmation that they have been paid off with a big cash award to dissociate themselves from you. Don't you know, your supervisor is still holding a grudge against you for notifying Upper Management (UM) that he was constantly clipping his overgrown toenails during work hours. If you walk off that job, he will have convinced the UMs that you are the problem employee, and not him. Don't be a fool, it's a set-up! Think about your rescue dog and your annual $150.00 cash award. Do something constructive with your time, like dedicating a recipe to express what you really feel about your boss–you can call it, "A Ruthless Meatball Head."

In every recipe creation, there is always an underline lesson to release a Home Cook's stress level. For this particular recipe, that lesson is, "It's prudent to release the tension in your hands on an innocent little meatball, than to go to jail for placing them around your supervisor's neck!"

Ingredients

2 ½ pound ground beef or chicken
1 cup whole wheat saltine crackers (finely crushed)
1 cup fresh parsley
3 egg whites
1 tsp. garlic powder

1 tsp. cayenne pepper
1 tsp. salt
1 tsp. black pepper
4 tbsps. olive or vegetable oil

Preheat a non-stick pan.

Step 1: In a medium mixing bowl, mix meat, egg whites, garlic powder, salt, black pepper, cayenne pepper, parsley, and saltine crackers. Roll or use a melon scooper to scoop up meatball. Transfer to a plate and set aside.

Step 2: Add oil and place approximately 6 to 7 meatballs in skillet to sauté; do not overcrowd the pan. Brown meatballs on both sides and transfer cooked meatballs to a clean plate with paper towel to remove excess oil. Repeat process until all meatballs are cooked.

Step 3: Clean pan with a paper towel to remove excess oil and add your favorite marinara sauce. Transfer meatballs back into pan. Cook for an additional 15 minutes and remove from heat. Make a meatball sandwich with cheese or serve as an appetizer. Make 16 meatballs.

Cooking Advisory Tip: When you present these meatballs at your next office party for your colleagues to be nice to you–it will allow you put all of your differences aside. Just be mindful, for job security purposes, do not disclose the title of this recipe. If a noisy colleague should ask, "What inspired you to make these delicious meatballs?," tell them, "There was an "Uncensored Home Cook" who had a short story to tell."

Hustling Truffles

My father use to always say, "Everybody is trying to make a hustle." I would have to say that statement is accurate if your full-time job is not totally taking care of your household expenses. Now, to relate hustling to criminal activity, that will depend on what your definition of hustling is. To help you figure it out, here are some examples of possible shady hustles:

* Paying $10.00 for a shot of liquor at the Shot House (SH), to help raise funds to replace the old banged up steel with a new and improve "gold plated" steel;
* Encouraging your child to sell homemade lemonade at $5.00 a cup–to ensure there is sufficient funds to pay off the family vacation;
* Purposely burning paying customers' hair out, at the salon, so they can become a patron at your basement salon–for a so called, "Restoration Hair Treatment (RHT);"
* Manipulating and threatening your subordinates to actually perform your $135,000 job and their $40,000 job as well; and
* Giving your college bound child "hush tuition" to pretend they are attending classes so your spouse can't find all of your hidden assets during the divorce proceedings.

If you are not conducting any of these hustles–than you should be able to have a good night sleep.

Fudge Ingredients

2 tbsps. condense milk
3 tsps. coconut rum

1 tbsp. cocoa powder
1 cup semi-sweet chocolate morsels

Fudge Sauce

½ cup semi-sweet morsels
1 tbsp. butter
3 tbsps. coconut rum
½ cup coconut flakes

Step 1: Pour 2 cups of water into a medium sauce pan and bring to a boil. Place a heat resistant bowl over the sauce pan (double boiler method). Add condense milk, coconut rum, cocoa powder, and chocolate morsels. Stir ingredients until melted. Remove from the heat and cool. Once fudge has cooled, place in refrigerator for 1 hour to set.

Step 2: Remove bowl of fudge from refrigerator and roll chocolate into 1 to 2 inch balls. Place on a sheet pan with a rack and set aside.

Step 3: Using the double boiler method again, add butter and morsels to melt. Remove bowl from sauce pan and add coconut rum. Set up 2 dreading stations, one for dipping the truffles and another for dreading the coconut flakes.

Step 4: Dip truffles in melted chocolate and then coconut flakes. Repeat process until all truffles have been dread. Place truffles back into refrigerator for 1 hour. Take out and enjoy this chocolate deliciousness. Make 12 truffles balls.

Cooking Advisory Tip: If you are able to speak without slurring after indulging in two of these truffles, this simply means the rum flavor will go undetected when it's served to a "Closet Drinker." As always, eat your truffles at home, and not behind the wheel.

SHAKEDOWN CHICKEN

Back in the day, if someone was threatening or causing harm to someone's kin folks, they would receive a good old-fashioned shakedown. What exactly is a shakedown? Well, a shakedown is merely a "Shaker" patiently waiting at dusk for a "Shakee" to step outside their place of residence to scare the hell out of them! Other than the Shakee becoming crossed-eyed from a 360 degree spin turn, their ego being diminished, and an expensive dry-cleaning bill, everybody pretty much walked away unharmed.

To carry-out a successful shakedown, a Country Statistical Study (CSS) had to be conducted exclusively by a countrified individual living in a rural area, to determine if all-purpose or self-rising flour could withstand a 30 minute paper bag shakedown. Factors like the diameter of a Shakee's head and greasy hair, had to be taken into consideration when determining which flour would be feasible. After careful consideration, all-purpose flour was selected for its staying power for giving the Shakee the appearance of a "disgruntle" ghost.

Whenever you decide to conduct a shakedown, please be patient for the "Shakee" to be transformed from a bully to a chicken. If the transformation should fail, you should always look at the bright side, "At least you will always have an abundance of brown paper bags for your next shakedown, and lots of all-purpose flour for future bake-off competitions."

INGREDIENTS

1 whole cut up chicken fryer (breast, wings, and legs)
2 tbsps. lemon juice

¼ cup vinegar

4 cups water

2 ½ cups whole wheat flour

1 tbsp. salt

1 tbsp. garlic powder

1 tbsp. black pepper

4 cups canola oil

1 large paper bag

Step 1: In a large bowl, soak chicken in the lemon juice, vinegar, and water for 25 minutes. Remove chicken from bowl and pat dry with paper towel. Set aside.

Step 2: Preheat Dutch oven with canola oil until it reaches 350° to 375° degrees or when the "test flour" sizzles when dropped into pan.

Step 3: In paper bag, add flour, salt, garlic powder, and black pepper. Add the chicken, close the bag, and initiate the shakedown (up and down). Place 3 pieces of chicken in Dutch oven 1 at a time to eliminate the temperature from dropping. Fry the chicken 5 to 6 minutes on each side, remove chicken from pan and drain excess oil on paper towel. Repeat process until all chicken has been fully cooked.

NOTE: If you want a "Sticky Bread Chicken Sandwich," while the chicken is still hot and greaseless, just slap it between two pieces of white bread and wrap it up in foil for 3 minutes. Once unwrapped, you will discover the deliciousness of "retro" eating!

Cooking Advisory Tip: If there's a Shaker in your family that is going through a difficult time because they were shaking down bullies on your behalf, prepare a delicious meal to show them your appreciation. Let them know, that without their courage and sacrifice, you would not have been able to graduate at the top of your class with a degree in "Criminal Law."

A $16 "Jerk" of a Turkey

I remember it like it was early this morning, it was October 23, 1999, and I had arrived home in the wee hours of the morning from a "pay preview" wrestling outing. As I drove my car between the chain link fences of my yard, I noticed a car zooming down the streets. I said to myself, "Who in world is out here besides me this time of the morning?" Within a second, there was a reply to the little voice in my head, that said:

Robber
"Don't move, give me the money!"

Country Lady
"Oh Father God, oh Father God, oh Father God!"
(Ignored the Robber–for a brief conversation with the
Heavenly Father.)

As the robbery was still in progress, I felt as though he was a little agitated with my screaming episodes. For some reason, his eyes began to shift up and down under his ski mask. After finally calming down from all that screaming, and realizing the Robber needed my cooperation–I decided he was much deserving of my last $16.00. As the money exchanged from my hands to his, one of the bills fell on my driveway, which caused us to have more dialogue with each other.

Robber
"Pick it up!"

Country Lady
"You pick it up!" You got the gun, "Who's in control here?"

(Country Lady was already stressed out enough from the robbery and was getting a little agitated with the Robber for trying to control the outcome of the robbery.)

Robber
(Robber adheres to the Country Lady's demands and picked the bill up and run!)

Country Lady
"Thank you Lord!"
(Country Lady realizes that the Heavenly Father had given her the courage to stand up to the nervous Robber, who's criminal activity would have been taken more seriously–if he was not wearing a t-shirt with "smiling" cartoon characters on it.)

As I jump out the car to run into the house to call the police, I finally realized that I had been robbed! I sure hope that Robber met his quota for that week, because I didn't have any more money to give him for another "love offering."

To eliminate potential reprisal from the "timid" Robber, the jurisdiction of where this robbery occurred will remain undisclosed. There is no need to cause any further embarrassment to that Robber, he's probably too ashamed to let his boys know a Country Lady had gotten him in check! I do hope and pray he did a good deed with that $16.00 that I was forced to give him–like buying a large bag of dog food to feed a homeless dog. Who knows, by now, he might have turned his life around to do legitimate outreach for the community. I hope so, because once he sees my face on the cover of this comedic cookbook, and he finds out that I acknowledge him with a recipe creation called, "A $16 "Jerk" of a Turkey," I might have to go into hiding again!

INGREDIENTS

    5 lb. turkey breast (cut into quarters)
    ½ habanero chili pepper (finely chopped)
    ½ tsp. thyme
    1 tsp. cayenne pepper
    ½ tsp. chili powder
    ½ tsp. all-spice
    1 tsp. sea salt
    1 tsp. basil
    1 tsp. dried rosemary
    1 tsp. garlic powder
    1 tsp. smoke paprika
    1 tsp. cumin
    ½ tsp. ground black pepper
    4 tbsps. canola oil (reserve 2 tbsp.)

Preheat oven to 350° degrees.

Overnight: In a food processor, combine habanero chili pepper, thyme, cayenne pepper, chili powder, all-spice, sea salt, basil, rosemary, garlic powder, smoke paprika, cumin, black pepper, and oil. Transfer mixture into a bowl, and generously rub the turkey. Marinate overnight to absorb all the "jerk" seasoning before cooking. Allow turkey to come to room temperature for 1 hour before cooking.

Oven: In a roaster, place jerk turkey breast in pan. Cover with lid and cook for 2 to 2 ½ hours. Use a meat thermometer to check the internal temperature; if the turkey breast has a 165° degree, it's fully cooked. Allow turkey to cool for 1 hour.

Broiler: With big knife, cut the turkey into 6 parts. Transfer on a sheet pan and turn the broiler on high. Monitoring the turkey breast in the broiler for approximately 5 minutes, to get a more authentic jerk flavor. Remove from broiler, and cover with foil for 30 minutes so juices can redistribute. Serve up and enjoy. Make 8 to 10 servings.

Cooking Advisory Tip: To prepare this recipe, it should cost you no more than $16.00. If the cost of these ingredients exceeds that amount, don't blame me, blame that Robber for not being smart enough to know a Country Lady always have a stash in her bra for emergencies. Maybe if he had control of the robbery, the recipe name would have been called, "A $36 "Jerk" of a Turkey."

CHAPTER 3

It's All About the Gravy: Don't be ashamed, hold your head down and sop it up!

• • •

Sopping Sausage Gravy

Like most laborers, my father was a hardworking man who valued a good meal. With those meals, for some reason, there was always gravy on his plate. He loved it so much, my mother had to incorporate it in every meal–to reduce her chances of being held in a "hostage situation" while me and my siblings were sound asleep. Believe me, there was so much gravy making on our farm, I swore I saw my mother retrieve gravy and onions from our milk cow. Who knows what I saw, I was a youngster–but it wouldn't be too far fetch if it did happen.

If you are planning to use this "Sopping Sausage Gravy" recipe, try not to criticize your family or friends when they begin to "sop" their plate. This would not be the time to be concern with table etiquette. If there's no one around to blackmail them with a video or selfie, and there's a biscuit in arms reach, just allow them to be themselves. You will not only save on water usage from the dishwasher, but you will begin the casting process for the first ever "Gravy Sopping" reality television show.

Ingredients

    1 roll pork sausage
    ½ cup of onions
    1 garlic clove
    ¼ cup of flour
    1 cup water
    ¼ tsp. salt
    ¼ tsp. black pepper

Step 1: In a large skillet, cook sausage until fully cooked. Remove sausage from pan and place on a plate with paper towels to remove excess grease (leave 2 tbsp. of the grease in pan) while disregarding leftover grease into grease can.

Step 2: To the pan, add onions and garlic; sauté until vegetables are translucent. Sprinkle flour and stir until color is a caramel brown. Gradually add water and whisk until smooth. Transfer sausage back into pan and cook for an additional 5 minutes, add salt and pepper to taste. Make 4 servings.

Cooking Advisory Tip: This is a good starter dish for the new love interest in your life. If they are a "Sopper," you will have a loving and lasting relationship, if they are not, be prepared to be in a relationship with a person who will never disclose their true identity.

Secret Sopper Chicken Livers & Gravy

As you prepare this gravy recipe and other gravy recipes in this chapter, it's inevitable that you will become a lifelong Sopper. When you enter into this adventure, please be cognizant of who you confide in. From my personal experience, I know what can happen if this type of information is leaked to "uppity" country folks who have forgotten where they came from. Please, don't take this advice the wrong way–I'm just trying to look out for the "Secret Sopper" who has contributed so much of their time to reduce the waste of food in this country. So I ask, "Are you a Sopper?" If so, be proud of it, and don't allow anyone to convince you to ever stop sopping!

Ingredients

1 (20 oz.) container chicken livers
1 ½ cup of all-purpose flour
1 medium size onion (finely chopped)
2 garlic cloves (finely chopped)
1 ½ tsp. seasoning salt
1 tsp. black pepper
1 cup of canola oil
1 ½ cup water

Step 1: Remove livers from container and rinse off. Pat dry with paper towel and set aside.

Step 2: In a large storage bag or bowl, add flour, seasoning salt, and black pepper. Add livers and coat with flour mixture.

Step 3: Preheat a skillet with oil, add floured livers and fry 1 minute on each side. Remove livers from pan and place on paper towel to remove access oil. Disregard grease into grease can (reserving 2 tbsp. of the oil in pan). Add onions and garlic and sauté until translucent.

Step 4: Place livers back into the pan and add water. Cook until the gravy has thickened. Plate up and serve over rice or with your favorite "sop bread." Make 4 servings.

Cooking Advisory Tip: A good gravy maker does not really need chicken stock for delicious gravy. Where I come from, there was no supply of chicken stock unless you were actually stewing a chicken. In short, the deliciousness of gravy comes from the leftover crumbs in the skillet and the chicken livers–this is what you call a little known "Make Do Generation (MDG)" fact.

Beef & Mushroom Gravy

Being the "Uncensored Home Cook," there is always a story behind a recipe creation. Sometimes a childhood memory will inspire that recipe creation. That would be the case of our farm bull, a.k.a., "Mr. Bully."

To describe Mr. Bully, I would say he was moody, territorial, and vindictive. Whenever my siblings and I had to go into the boob wired pastures to retrieve apples from the apple tree, for one of my mother's apples pies, it was mentally and physically draining. None of us knew which tree Mr. Bully would pop up from, shortly after his nap in the creek area of the pastures. What we knew for sure, it was nothing for Mr. Bully to do his infamous "pasture break" in the wee hours of the morning to tear up our senior neighbors' yard and return to our yard to chase my mother during one of her secretive cigarette breaks. This vicious bull was not mad because we chose to wear "orange" clothing versus "red" when we visited him–this bull was mad because we did not visit him when it was "pitch black" dark–which is the time he could really cause havoc. Lord knows, we didn't know if Mr. Bully was color blind or if he just wanted us to show him some affection by patting him on the head. All I know is, eventually my father showed Mr. Bully there was only room for one male bull on the farm–and this is where this story ends.

For confession purposes, I don't have too many nice things to say about Mr. Bully, but as an adult, I must find it in my heart to forgive him for harassing and tormenting my family and me on the farm. With that said, this recipe is dedicated to Mr. Bully, a misunderstood "old" bull–who just wanted some attention from a "young" heifer.

INGREDIENTS

1 lb. ground beef (93% lean & 7% fat)
1 (8 oz.) pkg. sliced baby bella mushrooms
¾ cup Marsala wine
1 medium onion (diced)
3 garlic cloves (finely chopped)
¼ tsp. garlic powder
¼ tsp. black pepper
1 ½ tbsp. flour
1 tsp. onion salt

Step 1: In medium mixing bowl, mix ground beef, garlic powder, salt, and black pepper.

Step 2: Preheat a large frying pan, add beef and thoroughly cook. Remove beef from pan and place on a paper towel. Disregard grease from pan into grease can (reserve 2 tbsp. of oil in pan).

Step 3: In the pan, add mushrooms, onions, garlic, and sauté until translucent. Sprinkle flour on the vegetables and stir. Slowly add wine and cook until sauce thickens. Transfer cooked hamburger back into pan and cook for an additional 12 minutes until gravy thickens. Remove from heat, plate up, and do some more sopping. Make 4 to 6 servings.

Cooking Advisory Tip: If there's a two-legged bully in your inner circle that keeps harassing and tormenting you, talk to someone with authority. Hopefully, they will be able to explain why you are being bullied and will take action to stop the bully from harming you any further. If this regulated advice is not working for you, just go to Chapter 2 of this cookbook, and take your pick of a "high risk" recipe or an idea from a storyline–to overwhelm Mr. or Ms. Bully with happiness.

Chicken Fried Steak w/ Carrot Gravy

As children, we were told to eat our carrots for good eye sight. For me, this was some good advice. By eating a voluminous amount of carrots, it has allowed me to witness some interesting occurrences in my lifetime–some of which I should have never been exposed to. For instance, I was able to see:

1. How Mother's rough handling of Father's feet was really a form of hostile foreplay;
2. The neighbor creeping across my lawn in the wee hours of the morning–to visit the other lonely neighbor while her husband was on official travel;
3. A lady who was not pregnant entering the grocery store but suddenly "knocked up" with a 20 pound turkey as she exited the grocery store; and
4. The real reason why the female colleague received a $10,000.00 pay raise.

Yes, I could blame all of these sightings on a poor little carrot, but that would be foolish of me. I need to come to terms with the real reason I chose to eat a voluminous amount of carrots. It was not because I want to have good eye sight, it's because I'm just too noisy!

STEAK

2 cubed steaks
¼ cup white wheat flour
½ tsp. onion powder
½ tsp. garlic powder

½ tsp. black pepper
¼ tsp. salt
1 cup canola oil

CARROT GRAVY

1 cup carrot juice
2 tbsps. white wheat flour

Preheat a skillet and add vegetable oil.

Step 1: Mix flour, onion powder, garlic powder, black pepper, and salt in a bowl. Toss cubed steaks in flour mixture and fry on both sides for approximately 2 minutes. Remove steaks from pan and drain on paper towel.

Step 2: Disregard grease from pan into grease can (reserve 2 tbsp. of oil in pan). In the frying pan, sprinkle 2 tbsp. of flour and stir for 2 minutes. Add carrot juice and whisk until thicken. Transfer steaks back to pan to absorb the carrot gravy. Garnish steaks with carrot gravy and serve. Make 2 servings.

Cooking Advisory Tip: Don't do carrots a disservice, if you have been a witness to something "shady," call a disowned relative to investigate the matter. Remember, if it was not for the carrot and noisy neighbors, "Neighborhood Watch" would be nonexistent.

Big Hand Biscuits

In order to have fluffy biscuits, the size of a Home Cook's hands is very crucial. Studies have proven, at least when my mother was making biscuits–that mothers who have big hands, not only had mouth-watering biscuits, they had discipline children and a stress free life. If you want to authenticate this study, do yourself a favor, and find a big handed individual with biscuit making capabilities. Trust me, you will have a life filled with happiness and peace.

Ingredients

2 cups self-rising flour (sifted into bowl)
4 tbsps. cold unsalted butter (cut into cubes)
¼ cup cold shortening
¾ cup buttermilk (shake well)
2 tsps. sugar

Preheat oven to 400° degrees.

Step 1: In a large mixing bowl, whisk together flour and sugar until incorporated. Add butter and shortening, using a pastry cutter, cut butter and shortening into flour until its looks clunky. Make a "well" in the middle of flour mixture and slowly add buttermilk. Work flour mixture into the buttermilk with hands until a dough is formed.

Step 2: Flour countertop and rolling pin with flour, roll out dough to your preference (less expansion will give you thicker biscuits). With a biscuit cutter (a glass is fine as well), cut out biscuits and place on sheet pan lined with parchment paper. Brush each biscuit with melted butter and cook biscuits for 18 to 20 minutes. Remove from oven.

Step 3: If biscuits are not brown enough for you, turn on broiler. Brush biscuits with butter again and place under broiler. Monitor the biscuits while in the broiler to ensure the desired brownness is achieved. Make 6 biscuits.

Cooking Advisory Tip: Have the family in the kitchen when the biscuits are released from the oven. Make sure they each have a butter knife to "slap" a dab of butter in that "cloud" of glory.

Piping Hot Rolls

This recipe is dedicated to the "Roll lovers" generation who had wonderful memories of their Mothers making homemade rolls from scratch. If you were part of this generation, you will be able to testify how your house was literally on "lockdown" during this wonderful creation process. It was a time, when a Mother didn't have to worry about her children whereabouts during the formation of this wonderful dough creation–because they were probably serving as bodyguards. Even the yard dog got in on the deal, by securing all entrances to the house so he too could be awarded a "hot" buttered yeast roll. Take my word for it, the taste and smell of "Piping Hot Rolls," will take you back to a time–you will never want to stop smelling.

Ingredients

> 2 packs dry yeast
> ½ cup sugar
> 1 egg
> 2 ¼ cups all–purpose flour
> 1 tbsp. of potato buds
> 2 ¼ cups of warm water
> 1 tsp. salt
> 2 sticks margarine (room temperature)
> 2 tbsps. melted butter (brushing rolls)

Preheat oven to 350° degrees.

Step 1: In a cup, allow the yeast to dissolve in hot water.

Step 2: In a large mixing bowl, mix flour, sugar, salt, and potato buds. Add margarine, egg, and yeast mixture. Mix ingredients together with a hand mixer or cake mixer. Add flour until a dough is firm. Divide dough in ½ and place in 2 separate bowls to rise for 1 to 1 ½ hour.

Step 3: After dough has risen in each bowl, flour hands, pick dough up and start shaping the rolls for the muffin pan or baking pan. Once the desired shape is formed, allow rolls to rise again for 1 to 1 ½ hours.

Step 4: Lightly brush the rolls with melted butter before placing in oven. Cook rolls for 30 to 35 minutes or until it becomes medium brown. Brush rolls again with melted butter 5 minutes before cooking time has ended. Make 12 dozen.

Cooking Advisory Tip: These rolls can be utilized for a "Mate Catcher (MC)," if you have run out of options for locking down a man. Just be mindful, stay clear of attracting a mate in the workplace, it could possibly jeopardize the "Flow of your dough!"

CHAPTER 4

Party Time, Is Anytime: Little teasers and pleasers that will sure get the party started.

• • •

Party Line Hot Wings

If you are over the age of 48, you will recall when neighbors shared a landline called the "Party Line." It was the telephone company way of forcing two or more parties to share a landline to ensure at least one of the designated parties would pay the bill. In other words, it was job security for person(s) who were employed at the telephone company.

As a party liner user, you had a reason to wake up every morning to pry into your neighbors' affairs. It gave you a sense of belonging to something important. Most of the best ear dropping sessions were early in the morning. If your ears were wax free, you would hear conversations like:

- The whereabouts to the Head moonshiner's steel operation in the county;
- How the county's "Remedy Person (RP)" concocted potions for adulterers who supposedly receive a rash from a poison ivy outbreak;
- How to hotwire a "Farm Use Truck (FUT)" to cross state lines to go to visit a country cousin up North; and
- The real reason the single lady down the road, with a house full of kids, was so eager to go to church–just to flaunt her kids in the gossiping church women faces.

Although the party line is no longer in existence, you should take the time to acquaint yourself with your neighbors. Who knows, you just might find one quality that you like about them.

INGREDIENTS

12 party wings
1 cup dill pickle juice
3 tbsps. butter
1 ½ cup hot sauce
½ cup of brown sugar
1 tbsp. garlic powder
1 tsp. salt
1 tsp. black pepper
1 ¼ cup blue cheese
Nonstick cooking spray

Preheat oven to 400° degrees.

Step 1: In a medium bowl or storage bag, add the garlic powder, salt, and black pepper. Spray each wing with nonstick cooking spray before placing on sheet pan with a rack. Place wings in oven and bake for 1 hour; remove from oven and cool.

Step 2: In medium sauce pan, melt butter and add dill pickle juice, hot sauce, and sugar. Stir until sauce has thickened, toss wings in sauce. Garnish with blue cheese. Serve with carrots, celery, or dill pickles. Make 4 servings.

Cooking Advisory Tip: If you do not have the right people in your party line, maybe you need to find some "new" wingettes to fly with.

Pleasers Pimento Cheese Shrimp Balls

There's not a person living who does not enjoy a tasty appetizer, which I prefer to call a "Pleaser." A Pleaser will please your stomach just before the main course is served. This methodology of indulging is not only for restaurateurs, it's for the Home Cook with little options to skip town. The Pleaser will become your best new friend while your family is waiting for you to exhaust yourself in the kitchen. If this is going on in your household, break the habit, and reclaim your catwalk. Think ahead, and eliminate your family from giving you the "stuck eye" look by preparing a Pleaser. This act of love will not only distract your family while you are relaxing at the day spa, it will guarantee the family dog will get their daily walk as well. Allow a Pleaser to work in your favor, for a life of freedom!

Ingredients

1 (12 oz.) container pimento cheese
1 cup shrimp (finely chopped & devein)
3 cups crunchy cheetos (finely crushed & reserving 1 cup)
½ cup small shell macaroni
½ cup skim milk
1 egg
2 cups flour
2 tbsps. butter
4 cups canola oil

Step 1: In small heated saucepan, melt butter, and cook shrimp for 1 minute. Remove from pan and transfer to a plate to cool. Set aside.

Step 2: In a large mixing bowl, mix pimento cheese, shrimp, shells, and 1 cup of the cheetos. Formulate 1 inch balls and refrigerate 1 to 2 hours or overnight.

Step 3: Set-up 3 dreading stations in this order: 1) Egg and milk mixture; 2) flour; and 3) 2 cups of cheetos. Dread the PPCSB in the order of: 1) Egg and milk; 2) flour; 3) egg and milk; and 4) final coat with cheetos. Repeat process until all PPCSBs are dreaded.

Step 3: Add oil to large frying pan and heat oil to 350° degrees or "test flour" in pan to see if it sizzle–that's an indication the oil is "hot." Place 5 to 6 PPCSB in the pan at a time; cook for 1 minute and quickly remove the PPCSB from oil (to ensure they will not break apart). Drain on a paper towel and start cooking your next batch until all PPCSBs are cooked. Make 20 PPCSB balls.

Cooking Advisory Tip: Utilize this Pleaser as a "resolution recipe" for your demanding life. Hopefully, your family will not catch onto your new found way of scaling back from cooking full course meals, unless they purchase this cookbook. By then, they wouldn't even care who coerce you into becoming a Runway model.

Roasted Pepper & Tomato Guacamole Dip

For most partygoers, guacamole dip is always out front for the introverted guests who have no intentions of getting their party on. If you are hosting a party for this subpopulation of guests, maybe you need to revamp your guacamole dip to attract some extraverted guests that will bring down the foundation of your house–while still coming back up for air. If this is your type of party, than you need to get up on it! If you don't release the party within you, no one will ever know you can "holla!" This is your time to shine, let's get the neighborhood jumping!

Ingredients

    2 avocados (sliced in quarters)
    3 garlic cloves (cut top, add oil, and wrap in foil)
    1 jar roasted bell peppers
    1 chipotle pepper
    3 sprigs of fresh basil
    1 (14.5 oz.) can petite diced tomatoes (drained)
    1 ½ tsp. olive oil
    ¼ tsp. salt
    ¼ tsp. black pepper

Preheat oven to 400° degrees.

Step 1: On a sheet pan, sprinkle olive oil on avocados and tomatoes. Add salt and pepper and place the wrapped garlic on sheet pan as well. Roast vegetables for approximately 30 minutes. Remove from oven and cool for 10 minutes.

Step 2: In a blender or food processor, transfer roasted vegetables, chipotle pepper, basil, and roasted bell peppers (plus 1/3 cup of its juice). Blend until smooth and pour in a bowl for dipping. Make 4 servings.

Cooking Advisory Tip: This dip can also serve as a sauce for your chicken, hamburgers, and fish.

Stuffed Tortilla Bell Peppers

During supper time or dinner time in your household, do you recall your parent(s) ordering you to, "Stop stuffing your mouth!" This command was probably verbalized because they were too afraid that two weeks of groceries would be gone within in one day. Of course for a youngster, this command was difficult to understand when the food was good and free. No matter how you swing it, sometimes it takes for you to become an adult before you can interpret what your parent(s) was really trying to tell you. Let me break it down for you, your parents was not really trying stop you from stuffing your mouth, they was trying to tell you, "Whenever you have a big spread of food presented buffet style, don't stuff your mouth, just stuff that storage bag!"

Ingredients

1 pound ground chicken
3 large bell peppers (halved)
1 ½ cup chunky salsa (medium)
1½ cup tortilla chip (finely chopped)
1 cup onions
2 garlic cloves
½ fresno pepper (optional)
½ jalapeno pepper
½ tsp. salt
½ tsp. black pepper
½ tsp. cumin
3 tbsps. olive oil or canola oil
Nonstick spray

Preheat oven to 350° degrees.

Filling:

Step 1: In a large skillet, sauté onions, garlic, and fresno/jalapeno pepper in oil. Add salt and black pepper and cook for 3 minutes. Add ground chicken and cumin; cook until pink is gone. Add salsa and cook for 8 minutes. Fold in tortilla chips and cook until sauce has thickened. Set aside.

Step 2: Split bell peppers in half. Spray sheet pan with nonstick spray and stuff each pepper with meat mixture. Place peppers in oven and cook for 35 minutes and remove from oven and cool for 5 minutes.

As toppers for the bell peppers, add sour cream, shredded lettuce, cheese, and more salsa. Use the extra tortilla chips for dipping. Make 6 servings.

Cooking Advisory Tip: If you feel the urge to stuff your mouth with these bell peppers, please wait until they are completely cool before you go for it!

Jalapeno Salmon Croquettes

When making any Teaser (appetizer), it's a great opportunity to show your guest that being broke does not mean a hostess has to compromise the ingredients in their food. If you are adventurous, a risk taker, and not afraid of having a permanent "fishy" smell on your hands, this is the recipe that will give you all that, and some more.

Ingredients

1 (14.75 oz.) can pink salmon
1 jalapeno pepper (finely diced)
15 saltine crackers (crushed)
1 tsp. cilantro paste
1 tbsp. taco seasoning
2 egg whites
3 cups canola oil
Salt to taste

Step 1: Drain salmon juice from can. Remove bones and skin.

Step 2: In a large mixing bowl, add salmon, jalapeno pepper, crackers, cilantro paste, taco seasoning, and egg whites. Mix well with hands and form 12 croquettes.

Step 3: Preheat frying pan, add oil and sautéed croquettes for 5 minutes or until preferred crispiness is achieved. Remove croquettes from pan and transfer to a plate with paper towel to remove excess oil. Serve up and enjoy. Make 4 servings.

Cooking Advisory Tip: Try dipping these croquettes in my "Horseradish Pea Hummus" for a tasty indulgence.

Turkey in a Throw

Whenever there is a "Pig in a Blanket" being served at a party, he is always kept warm in a blanket for starving guests. Sometimes if the guests are late arriving to the party, the pig will get over-heated and start to lose his coloration. It is at this time, the pig will become furious that he had to wait so long to be transferred to a cooler place. If this is the norm for you, and the pig that has given a generous amount of his time at your parties–you should send him on a Caribbean vacation to relieve him from his stress. When he leaves, ensure him that he has job security. Convey to him, that his rival, "Turkey in a Throw" will be lying on a platter on his behalf. If your guest should inquire about the pig where-abouts, tell them, "He needed some time to find himself."

Ingredients

    1 sheet frozen puff pastry
    12 turkey links (room temperature)
    ½ cup flour

Preheat oven to 350° degrees.

Step 1: On the countertop and rolling pin, sprinkle flour. Roll out dough, and cut into 3 inch squares. Wrap dough from the end of the turkey link to midway. Continue until all turkey links are wrapped.

Step 2: On a sheet pan, add parchment paper and place turkey throws in pan. Bake 12 to 15 minutes or until pastry is golden brown. Place on a platter and eat up! Make 4 servings.

Cooking Advisory Tip: If you have a guest who's in the "Pork Rehabber Program (PRP)," for persons who are transitional away from pork, and don't have a teaser to replace their pork withdrawals, this would be a good appetizer to possibly get them off the pork wagon.

CHAPTER 5

Grilling w/o Heals: Strategic grilling techniques for the "Wannabe Griller" who's too afraid their synthetic hair will catch on fire.

• • •

BACKSTABBING RIBS

Have you ever been backstabbed in your back until your ribs felt the pain? If you have, then you should be wigless by now. If you have not experienced this "dramatic episode" in your life, keep on living, it will be coming to a theater near you. When it occurs, it's okay to release those tears for approximately 10 minutes. After that, regroup, and take this as confirmation that you have found your calling of being a "Master Griller (MG)"–who is able to grill high flamed foods while wearing a wig. See, how the "shame" from gossip can lead you straight into your destiny.

RIBS

1 Full rack Saint Louis Ribs

DRY RUB

1 tbsp. garlic powder
1 tbsp. onion powder
1 tsp. cayenne pepper
1 tbsp. cumin
1 tbsp. smoky paprika
1 tbsp. brown sugar
1 tbsp. salt
1 tbsp. black pepper

Marinate: Remove membrane from ribs. Rub ribs with dry rub ingredients (garlic/onion powder, cayenne pepper, cumin, smoky paprika, salt, pepper and sugar) and place in a paper bag overnight in the refrigerator. Take ribs out of refrigerator and allow them come to room temperature 1 hour prior to cooking.

Vinegar & Margarine Wet Sauce (Oven)

½ cup of white vinegar
3 tbsps. margarine

Microwave margarine in a bowl, stir in vinegar. Set aside.

Oven: In a preheated 350° degree oven, place ribs on a sheet pan with rack. Bush ribs with vinegar and margarine wet sauce. Cover ribs with foil and cook for 30 minutes. Brush ribs with another coat of sauce and decrease oven temperature to 300° degrees for an additional 1 ½ hour of cooking time.

Barbecue Sauce (Grill)

1 cup of ketchup
1 cup apple cider vinegar
2 tbsp. Worchester sauce
½ cup brown sugar
1 tsp. onion powder
1 tsp. garlic powder
1 tbsp. cumin
1 ginger root knob (place in sauce)
2 tbsp. sweet orange marmalade
¼ tsp. cayenne pepper

Barbecue Sauce: In medium saucepan, combine all barbecues sauce ingredients (ketchup, apple cider vinegar, Worchester sauce, brown sugar, onion powder, garlic powder, cumin, ginger, orange marmalade and cayenne pepper). Bring to a boil, reduce heat and simmer uncovered for 1 ½ hour (sauce can be cooked a day ahead).

Grilling: Using an INDIRECT method, place briquettes on ONE side of grill and ribs on the opposite side. Fill tin pan with 2 cups of vinegar and 1 tbsp. of cumin. Place pan directly underneath the middle of the grate to ensure ribs will stay moist during grilling.

Brush ribs with barbecue sauce when 1st placed on grill. Smoke ribs for approximately 3 hours. Brush another coat of the barbecue sauce the last 10 minutes of cooking time.

Remove ribs from grill, tint with foil, and rest for about 30 minutes before indulging. Serve 2 to 4 persons.

Cooking Advisory Tip: If you have been backstabbed by someone who you trusted, send them a "CERTIFIED" letter and give them a visual of their darkest secrets they shared with you. This action will not only be therapeutic for you, it will show the backstabber how it feels to have their darkest secrets splattered on a piece of paper that they actually "SIGNED" for!

Bedroom Slippers Grill Chicken

Ladies and Gentlemen, if you want try your hands at grilling, I have a grilling experience for you. This recipe is so easy, you will be able to grill in your bedroom slippers–there's no need to get all dressed up for the day. All you have to do is, get out of bed, and thoroughly wash your hands and face before grilling. This act will give you a "B+" in personal hygiene, and ensure that you have awakened at the right house.

Ingredients

1 (4 lb.) chicken fryer
¼ cup margarine
1 cup white distilled vinegar
2 tbsps. garlic powder
1 tsp. salt
1 tsp. tsp black pepper

Marinate: In a medium bowl, season chicken with garlic powder, salt, and black pepper. Marinate chicken in refrigerator overnight. Remove the chicken from the refrigerator and allow 1 hour for chicken to come to room temperature.

Basing: In a microwavable cup, melt margarine and remove from microwave. Pour vinegar in cup and mix well. Set aside.

Grilling: Set up the grill using INDIRECT method (briquettes on EACH side of grill pot) Light grill according to your grill instructions. When briquettes are white, the chicken will be ready to grill. Place the chicken in the middle of grill rack and base chicken every

30 minutes with vinegar and margarine sauce. Grill 1 ½ hour or until there is an internal temperature of 165° degrees.

Once the chicken is fully cooked, take off the grill and cover with foil. Rest chicken for about 25 minutes before indulging. Serve 4 to 6 people.

Cooking Advisory Tip: If this is your first time lighting a charcoal grill, please refrain from wearing a synthetic wig because everybody knows synthetic will burn faster than human hair. This is a bedroom slipper recipe, not a "Hair on Fire While Grilling" recipe.

Smoke Houser's Meat Brisket

Back in the early '70s, in some rural areas of the south, there's a possibility that you had an "active" wood stove because your father was too cheap to buy a gas stove. If this was a relatable moment in your household, there's a possibility you or someone you knew, had a "smoke meat" aroma embedded in their skin and clothing. If you knew of such person(s), than you were residing with a functional "Smoke Houser (SH)."

Most expert SHs knew how to generate enough smoke to run their uncontrollable kids out of the house. This was mainly because they just wanted some quiet time to take a nap. Usually, this plan was workable, until the next door neighbor realized the SH was scamming her to babysit her unruly kids for free.

If you are a hardworking SH or know of someone who is still smoking their kids out of the house, this recipe is dedicated to you. Thanks for getting up early in morning and keeping the fire going so your family could have a delicious hot meal–there will always be a special place in my heart for you.

Brisket

1 (2 lb.) Brisket
1 tbsp. black pepper
1 tbsp. salt
1 tbsp. garlic powder
1 tsp cayenne pepper
1 tbsp. cumin

SAUCE

> 1 ½ cup of ketchup
> 2 chipotle peppers
> ½ cup of vinegar
> ½ cup of brown sugar
> 1 jar roasted bell peppers (puree)
> 1 tbsp. of grape jelly

Marinate: In a large bowl, rub the brisket with pepper, salt, garlic powder, cayenne powder, and cumin. Marinate 5 hours or overnight in refrigerator. Take brisket out refrigerator and allow brisket to come to room temperature for 1 hour before grilling.

Basing: In a small bowl, add ketchup, chipotle peppers, vinegar, brown sugar, roasted pepper and grape jelly.

Grilling: Using INDIRECT method (briquettes on EACH side of grill pot), place brisket in middle of grill rack, base with sauce, and smoke for 4 hours. Base the brisket 30 minutes before cooking time has completed. Remove from grill and tint brisket with foil for 20 minutes to allow the juices to redistribute. Cut against the grain and serve over a nice warm bun with your favorite cold slaw. Make 8 to 10 servings.

Cooking Advisory Tip: Remember always consult with your local fire department or a "Moonshiner Analyst (MA)," on how to smoke meat without having too much choking and coughing.

Grill Dill Pork Chops

There's nothing like a delicious juicy grilled pork chop. It's what I like to call, "Some good eating." If you want some TRUTH to get all up in you, than you need to get out of that chair, and get some pork chops on that grill, to get some of that LYING out of you!"

Ingredients

2 thick center cut pork chops
3 diced kosher dill pickles (reserve ½ cup of pickle juice)
½ tsp. garlic powder
1 tsp. black pepper
¼ cup canola oil
1 gallon zip lock bag

Marinate: In a zip lock bag, rub chops with garlic powder and black pepper. Add oil and pickles with juice. Marinate chops in refrigerator overnight.

Take pork chops out refrigerator and let them come to room temperature for approximately 1 hour before grilling.

Grilling: Use the DIRECT heat method (place briquettes in center of grill). Place foil over grid and place pork chops in the middle of the grid. Close grill top and cook pork chops 8 to 12 minutes on each side. Remove pork chop from grid and cover pork chops with foil for 20 minutes to allow the juices to redistribute. Plate up and get down with the get down. Make 2 to 4 servings.

Cooking Advisory Tip: For the first time griller who will be overseeing these pork chops, may I suggest you "flip" them precisely at the time allotted. Which means, "Don't be getting into a heavy texting message session or talking on the phone." Learn to respect the art of grilling–to reduce your chances of the fire department paying an "uninvited" visit to your house!

GRILL ROASTED PEPPER CORN ON THE COB

When it comes to grilling vegetables, it can be a bit challenging–almost as challenging as trying to grill in 4 inch heels. That's why I recommend corn on the cob for your first time grilling experience. When grilling corn on the cob, you will be able to use the "husk" as a storage place for your seasonings, as well as a protector to lock in the flavors. Do yourself a favor, and try your hand at grilling a vegetable, it will give you much appreciation of what comes from the earth.

INGREDIENTS

4 Corn on the cobs
1 stick margarine or butter (room temperature)
1 cup roasted red pepper from jar (pat dry and finely chopped)

Step 1: Pull husk away from corn and remove silk.

Step 2: In medium bowl, mix together margarine or butter with roasted pepper. Massage the mixture all over the corn. Afterwards, pull husk back over the corn and wrap corn with foil. Poke holes in foil for venting and set aside.

Step 3: Set up the grill using INDIRECT method (place briquettes on each side of grill pot) Place the corn in the middle of grill rack and grill for 25 minutes. Remove from grill and add your season of preference. Make 4 servings.

Cooking Advisory Tip: This corn will exercise your teeth when indulging–make sure you have some dental sticks or a tree limb to "pick" those corn kernels between your teeth. Also, you might want to find a corner spot on the patio because the corn juice and seeds will have you looking like you have the "chickenpox."

CHAPTER 6

A Be Kind Meal: Food indulgences that will inspire you to be kind to someone in a special way.

• • •

Corn, Toe, & Bunion Chowder

Have you ever heard someone say, "You put your foot in this?" If so, don't be alarmed, this statement is just to commend the cook for putting their heart and soul into a meal. Now, some of you might believe the Home Cook actually put their foot into the pot. Well, it depends on who you ask. If you're into a tasty indulgence whereas it requires one to place their foot into food, the answer would be "yes," if not, the answer would be "no." Whatever your response is, as long as you thoroughly wash your corns, toes, and bunions, where you immerse your foot is your personal business.

As a risk taker, you might want to conduct your own independent study for this chowder. Just put a tablespoon of chowder on the aforementioned foot parts, in a timely manner, and see what happens. Of course, there's a possibility you will need the assistance of a Trustee to partake in this study. Once this study is completed, you will not only become eager to visit the grocery store, you will be more than willing to purchase a year supply of chowder ingredients for your next independent study.

Ingredients

4 Corn on the cobs or 3 (11 oz.) cans of corn (no salt added)
½ cup vegetable stock
½ cup heavy cream
½ habanero chili pepper (optional)
1 jalapeno pepper (finely chopped)
1 onion
1 tsp. garlic powder
1 tsp. salt

1 tsp. black pepper
2 tbsps. sugar
2 tbsps. butter or margarine

Step 1: Preheat pan with butter or margarine. Add peppers, on-ions, garlic powder, salt, pepper, and sugar, sauté until translucent. Add corn, vegetable stock, and heavy cream; bring to a boil for 20 minutes.

Step 2: Ladle 1 cup of chowder from pot and transfer to a blender and puree until smooth. Pour pureed chowder back into sauce pan and allow chowder to cook for another 30 minutes. Serve with a piece of blacken fish or smoke kielbasa sausage. Make 4 servings.

Cooking Advisory Note: If your bunion has become problematic and your podiatrist has not yet approved you for a bunion removal, please inform the Trustee of this critical information prior to the adherence of this chowder. We do not want the bunion and big toe to become a deterrent for the Trustee–this is supposed to be a joyful experience–not a death sentence.

FRYING PAN HOE CAKES

If you were born in 1745, you would be able to confirm the origin of "hoecakes." Some people believe hoecakes were cooked in an iron pan or on the blade of a garden hoe. Personally, I can only attest to my mother cooking hoe cakes in a cast iron skillet because a garden hoe was not feasible for a family of six. The most use we got out of a garden hoe was, chopping the weeds in the fields, and chasing away my father's trouble making friends!

INGREDIENTS

    1 cup self-rising corn meal
    ¾ cup buttermilk
    ¼ cup sour cream
    1 ¼ tsp. sugar
    4 tbsps. margarine
    2 eggs

Preheat a nonstick pan with margarine.

Step 1: In a large mixing bowl, mix corn meal, buttermilk, sour cream, eggs, and sugar. Mix well until all ingredients have been incorporated.

Step 2: Once pan is hot, slowly ladle the batter into skillet. Cook cakes until holes are formed on top. Flip over and cook other side until desired brownness. Plate up and enjoy. Make 8 servings.

Cooking Advisory Tip: Other than serving these hoe cakes alongside fried fish, try topping the hoe cakes with the sweetness of corn syrup or grape jam. Remember, there is always a way to settle a sweet craving.

Road Trip Peanut Brittle

Almost everyone has been on a road trip at least once in their lifetime. Whether you were visiting your grandma's house, or running from the law in a high speed car chase, you have probably been on a road trip. My recollection of a road trip was driving down country roads, in unknown territories, in search of a Country store with goodies. Besides my savory goodies of pickle eggs and pig feet, I would say, the peanut brittle was my sweet goody. To me, it looked like a road map with warts wrapped up in cling wrap that took over 30 minutes to remove from bondage. It was not an inconvenience for me, once it was unwrapped. When that brittle attached itself to my teeth, I knew there was going to be enough sugar in me–to make my parents want to leave me at the Country store where I bought it.

Memories of those road trips adventures will always have special place in my heart. If I had to call it, the lesson I learned from eating peanut brittle on those road trips would have to be, "Never underestimate the strength of leftover cling wrap from a peanut brittle in the back seat of a car–my parents could probably attest to that!"

I hope this recipe has inspired you to take a road trip with your family, to create some memorable moments. Who knows, you just might discover a small business owner who's awaiting your arrival.

Ingredients

1 ½ cup roasted peanuts
1 tsp. vanilla extract
1 cup light corn syrup
½ cup sugar

¼ cup water
1 tbsp. butter
¼ tsp. baking soda

Step 1: Place parchment paper on sheet pan and set aside.

Step 2: In a medium sauce pan, combine syrup, sugar, water, butter, and extract. Stir ingredients until sugar has dissolved. Bring mixture to a boil and cook mixture on medium heat for approximately 25 to 30 minutes without stirring or until temperature reaches 280° F on a candy thermometer.

Step 3: Fold in peanuts and stir while cooking for 12 to 15 minutes to ensure peanuts will not burn. When mixture has a caramel color and separates into threads, remove sauce pan from stovetop and stir in baking soda. Immediately pour mixture on sheet pan lined with parchment paper. Spread out mixture, cool for approximately 20 minutes, and break into pieces. Make 6 to 8 servings.

Cooking Advisory Tip: This brittle should not be eaten if your teeth are in a fragile state. If you are having these problems, consult with your dentist before getting down on this brittle.

Savory Oven Thighs

In today's world, a single Home Cook must utilize her knowledge of food to determine if a relationship will last. For an example, prior to you secretly meeting a man from a dating website at an undisclosed location, you should inquire about his food of choice. His response will determine if you will make it home safely or if he will be a cheap date. If he reveals he is a meat and potato man, there's a 90% chance, he's in search of a wife who will prepare him three daily full course meals. Therefore, if you consider yourself to be a "high maintenance" woman, this man will not be the man you will be taking home to meet your parent(s).

As for me, the food analogy with relationships began when my ex-boyfriend confessed to me that he was a thigh man. From the beginning of the relationship, he was always complimenting and gazing at my thighs. I should have known right then and there, it was going to be another high speed chase, and a considerable amount of bacon grease crumbs to keep my thighs exfoliated.

As time went on, the chases became unbearable–I was unwillingly losing weight. I wanted to call the authorities, but there was no written law for a City man chasing a Country Lady who was exfoliating her thighs with bacon grease crumbs to keep her man. Eventually, I got tired, and I decided to go back to an ingredient that my mother used to run my father away from her. That ingredient was none other than, good old fashion "fatback" grease. The next time my ex-boyfriend came around me, there was no running, no screaming, and no scratching. That encounter was the last time I ever saw him again. I guess the truth was there the whole time, but I was just too out of breath to realize–he preferred bacon over fatback.

If there was a lesson to take away from this story, it would be, "If you are dating a thigh man, don't remove the bacon grease can from the stove, unless you are planning to permanently cook with it!"

INGREDIENTS

6 chicken thighs
6 tbsps. wheat flour (1 tablespoon per chicken for even distribution)
1 tbsp. thyme
1 tbsp. oregano
1 tbsp. garlic powder
1 tbsp. black pepper
1 tsp. of salt
Nonstick spray

Preheat oven to 400° degrees.

Step 1: In a gallon freezer bag, add thyme, oregano, black pepper, garlic powder, and salt. Add chicken to the bag and massage spices into chicken until herbs are well distributed.

Step 2: Add the flour to bag and massage flour into chicken. Place chicken on sheet pan with rack. Spray each thigh with nonstick spray and place chicken in oven to cook for 1 hour 15 minutes for crispiness. Make 6 servings.

Cooking Advisory Tip: This is recipe is for the Home Cook who has removed the grease can from the stove for fire hazard purposes.

Now, that you will no longer need to use leftover bacon grease for frying, you can now market it as natural bacon grease exfoliate for woman attempting to keep their mate on lockdown.

White Russian Tiramisu Parfait

To do something fancy for my 1st authored comedic cookbook, and prove that I can be elegant, I thought it would be great idea to create a Tiramisu recipe for the reader who wanted to be lifted up a little higher. It is my hope, that your impression of me will not be solely on the liquor content of the "expresso mixture" for this recipe, but more so for the deliciousness of the parfait. Please don't judge me, I only recall "taste testing" three table-spoon of vodka to ensure accuracy for this recipe–"I think!"

Sponge Cake

1 cup cake flour (sifted into batter)
1 cup confectionary sugar
½ cup granulated sugar
1 tsp. vanilla extract
6 eggs (separate egg whites)

Preheat oven at 350° degrees.

Step 1: Place egg whites into a large mixing bowl. Beat with a hand mixer; gradually add the confectionary sugar. While still beating the eggs, add the vanilla extract. Once peeks are formed, stop beating the mixture. Set aside.

Step 2: In a medium mixing bowl, add ½ cup sugar to egg yolks and beat until it's a light yellow color. Fold the yolks into egg whites. Do not over mix.

Step 3: Sift flour into egg mixture. Slowly fold flour into mixture until incorporated.

Step 4: Pour batter on a sheet pan and bake for 20 minutes. Take out of oven and cool on rack.

Mascarpone Filing

1 container mascarpone cheese
¼ cup confectionary sugar
6 egg yolks

Expresso Mixture

2 tbsps. coffee liquor
3 tbsps. vodka
½ cup heavy or light cream
½ cup coffee

Step 5: In a large bowl, whisk egg yolks, mascarpone cheese, and sugar until fully incorporated. Set aside.

Step 6: In mixing cup, mix coffee, coffee liquor, vodka, and cream.

Step 7: Add 2 tbsp. of espresso mixture to mascarpone filing.

Assembly

Step 8: To assembly the parfait, use a biscuit cutter (a glass is fine as well) to form a circle shape for the parfait.

Assembly the parfait with: 1) store bought cool whip; 2) cake; and 3) mascarpone filling. Repeat process until the whip cream garnishes the parfait. Make 4 servings.

Cooking Advisory Tip: Fold in some prepared instant chocolate pudding with whip cream for the first layer of the Tiramisu–if you really want the chocolate to "marry" the coffee liquor.

OVERWHELMED OMELET

In our everyday day life of hustle and bustle, we sometimes get overwhelmed with trying to accomplish all of our responsibilities within 24 hours. That alone could lead one to be resentful or frustrated. It could also make you realize that you are not that overwhelmed, and there are people out there who wish they were as overwhelmed as you. For instance, they might wish they were overwhelmed with:

* Being able to buy their ungrateful children designer apparel, the latest electronics, and whatever they whine for;
* Having the means to maintain a 24 hour surveil lance schedule to stalk the love of their life;
* Having a 5,000 square footage house to summons their spouse to another bedroom because of their "earthquake" snoring; and
* Maintaining a lavish life style just to be part of an inner circle of narcissistic friends, who probably won't even bring you a piece of "souse meat" before the "final" call.

Yes, if you can relate to any of the aforementioned "situations," you might be overwhelmed. But if you can't relate, just go into the kitchen, cook a meal, and become a "Food Fairy (FF)" to someone who is not as overwhelmed as you.

INGREDIENTS

½ cup bake potato filling
½ cup sausage or turkey sausage (cooked)
1 cup smoke gouda cheese
½ cup white cheddar cheese

4 eggs
¼ cup bell pepper
¼ cup onion
¼ cup porta bella mushrooms
4 tbsps. oil

Step 1: Preheat large non-stick skillet with oil, add bell pepper, onions, and mushrooms and sauté for 3 minutes.

Step 2: In a mixing bowl, mix eggs, potatoes, sausage, and cheeses. Pour mixture over vegetables in pan. Take spatula to go around the omelet to make sure it does not stick while "shaking" the pan so the bottom of the omelet will not stick as well. Once the omelet edges are firm, fold 1 side of the omelet over to the other side (it should look like a half moon). Garnish with grated smoke gouda cheese. Make 2 servings.

Cooking Advisory Tip: This omelet can be eaten anytime you feel too overwhelmed to cook a full course meal.

FLIGHTY CHICKEN SALAD

On your first plane ride, "Where you informed by the Airline Stewardess that the food being served was free?" If you were a 25 year old, naïve Country girl, on her way to Naples, Florida, in the spring of 1991, you were probably not informed.

The day I board the plane was bright and sunny. I was so excited to get on that plane to be in close proximity to heaven. I imagine it was going to be an enclosed roller coaster ride without the flipping. Since the airport was so overwhelming to maneuver, I quickly received my ticket from the ticket counter so I could follow the Caucasian man in front of me–he seemed confident in where he was going. He took me straight to security to ensure I would not harm him. Eventually, he led me to the gate where the plane would be departing. After waiting 30 minutes, we finally board the plane to take off into the clouds.

Once we were acclimated in the sky, I recall, the Airline Stewardess pushing a silver magician box down the aisle way. When the box arrived at my seat, she slowly tilted her head, put on a fake smile, and asked, "Would you prefer chicken or beef?" Being a prepared Country girl who already had a "sticky" white bread fried chicken sandwich in her purse, I politely told her, "No thank you, but thanks for the offer." My quick response was out of fear that she was going to take away my chicken sandwich. If that was not the case, maybe she wanted confirmation that African Americans do prefer chicken over beef. Who knows what kind of survey that Airline Stewardess was conducting, all I know was–my stomach was making loud noises, and it was time for me to "get down" on that chicken sandwich.

Eventually the Airline Stewardess came back around to disseminate the passengers' meals. As she proceeded to give each passenger their meals, I noticed that none of them were giving up any funding. It was at this point, I realized the meal was free. Once this visual was apparent, I felt really bad that I had misjudged the nice Airline Stewardess–who just wanted to ensure my growling stomach would not disturb the passengers on the plane.

If I had to take away a learning experience from my 1st plane ride, it would have to be, "If you take a homemade chicken sandwich on a plane, in a greasy brown bag, don't be ashamed to remove it from your purse, to offer a noisy Airline Stewardess a piece of it!"

INGREDIENTS

2 cups rotisserie chicken (chopped)
1 tbsp. red onions (finely chopped)
1 tsp. lemon juice
½ cup miracle whip
1 tsp. garlic powder
½ tsp. black pepper

Step 1: Place chicken in a mixing bowl and squeeze lemon juice. Add red onions, garlic powder, black pepper, and miracle whip. Mix well and serve on a bun or with your favorite cracker. Make 4 servings.

Cooking Advisory Tip: This chicken salad is ideal to "sneak" on the plane if you are reluctant to make an effort to fry up a "Sticky White Bread Chicken Sandwich" unlike the "Freedom Pioneers (FP)" before us. This recipe is dedicated to your struggle for providing me the opportunity to have my Civil Rights–hooray for the chicken!

Sweet Potato Patty Cakes

When I became a young lady, my interest in boys was no longer a hidden secret. I began to wear tight fitting clothes that prevented me from breathing and heavy make-up that would make me unidentifiable if my body was discovered on a dark dirt road. With all that going on, I still needed to know how to handle a boy attempting to do something he had no business doing. To get the answer I needed, there was only one person that I knew, who could explain how to deal with this upcoming encounter, that person was none other than, my mother.

The day I had gotten the courage to talk to my mother about boys was very nerve reckoning for me. I recall it being around supper time and my mother was already preoccupied with meeting my father's food challenge deadline. While she was moving swiftly to plate up the food, I decided this would be the perfect time to ask the question that could break me into womanhood. So, I took a deep breath, smell underneath my arms to wake me up, and I ask the question, "Momma, what should I do if a boy tries to get after me?" For some reason, she maintained her pace in preparing for the food challenge. I posed the question again, but with a louder volume. This time, my mother came to a halt. She walked over to me, pressed her face close to mines, looked me in one of my eyes, and said, "If a boy tries to get after you, play patty cake!" Her response was not the answer I was expecting. It was difficult to determine if my mother wanted me to actually play patty cake with the little boy, or if she just wanted my hands to be preoccupied–so the little boy could play patty cake on me. The one-way discussion with my mother, had confused me even more.

If there was a lesson from my only "Birds and the Bees" discussion with my mother, I would have to say, it was, "Never ask your mother about how to handle boys if you are not prepared for a visual of your parents playing patty cake in the dark!"

INGREDIENTS

2 medium size sweet potatoes (diced)
½ cup granola cereal (pulse in Food Processor)
1 tsp. carrot/orange juice
4 egg whites
¼ cup flour
¼ tsp. nutmeg
2 tbsps. light brown sugar
3 tbsps. unsalted butter
1 tsp. rum extract
1 tsp. vanilla extract
1 tbsp. canola oil

Step 1: In a medium sauce pan bring water to a boil. Place sweet potatoes in water and boil for 20 minutes or until fork soft. Drain water in a colander and cool.

Step 2: Place potatoes in a blender or food processor to puree. Transfer potato puree into mixing bowl and add vanilla/rum extract, nutmeg, brown sugar, carrot/orange juice, and egg whites. Mix all ingredients by hand until patties are formed. Set aside.

Step 3: In the food processor, pulse together cereal and flour. Transfer flour mixture to mixing bowl. Coat each patty in flour mixture and set aside.

Step 4: Preheat a nonstick pan, add oil and butter. Add patties and sauté 4 to 5 minutes on each side. Remove patties from pan and transfer to paper towel to remove excess oil. Make 6 patties.

Cooking Advisory Tip: This is a good recipe for couples who want to play patty cake for a bonding experience.

CHAPTER 7

Something Different: Rehabbed recipes that could make or break a Home Cook's confidence.

• • •

Experimental Meatloaf

If you are a newlywed Home Cook who is reluctant to cook a meal because you are too afraid of your mother-in-law's criticism, this meatloaf recipe will give you the confidence to possibly woman up!

During the experimenting process of making this meatloaf, you will need to handle the ground meat with tender loving care. This will allow the meatloaf to melt in your mother-in-law's mouth for whenever you decide to invite her over for a free "taste test." Be mindful, her feedback could possibly make or break your confidence as a Home Cook. Whatever happens, don't spend too much of your energy trying to please her. Instead, focus on more critical matters, like, how to fatten your man up, so he can get into those tight jeans you bought for him on your honeymoon night!

When all is said and done, once your mother-in-law realizes you can burn in the kitchen, she will finally be relieved of her duties as the "back-up" Home Cook for your husband.

Ingredients

1 pound ground meat (beef or chicken)
½ cup smoke beef kielbasa sausage (remove casing & finely chop)
½ cup herb seasoned stuffing
½ cup chopped onions (pulse in food processor or finely chopped)
3 egg whites
1 tsp. fresh parsley
1 tsp. kosher salt
1 tsp. course black pepper
Nonstick spray

SAUCE

¼ cup of ketchup
¼ tsp. chipotle juice
1 tsp. Dijon mustard
Pinch of cumin seasoning

Preheat oven to 375° degrees.

Step 1: In a small bowl, pour egg whites over stuffing to absorb for 5 minutes.

Step 2: Transport stuffing mixture to mixing bowl. Add ground meat, kielbasa sausage, onions, salt, black pepper, and parsley. Shape meatloaf into an oval shape. Spray casserole dish with nonstick spray and place meatloaf in a baking dish.

Step 3: In a mixing bowl, combine ketchup, chipotle juice, mustard, and cumin together. Spread sauce over the meatloaf and bake for covered for 30 minutes and uncovered for 30 minutes. Remove meatloaf from oven and rest for 5 minutes before serving. Make 6 to 8 servings.

Cooking Advisory Tip: For leftover meatloaf, toast on each side for 3 minutes in a nonstick pan and add your favorite cheese. Slap it between some toasted bread, and go to town!

Sunrise Gumbo

Have you ever taken the time to see the sunrise in the morning? If you have not, you should try embracing the natural light that awakens you every day. Once you do, you will realize the beautification of it all–is priceless. Who knows, you might finally see your innocent teenager sneaking in the house just before your alarm clock goes off. That's only the half of it, there's a lot more going on in your neighborhood, if you just take the time to get out of your bed, to see the sunrise.

Ingredients

6 boneless skinless chicken thighs (cut into ¼ quarters)
1 ½ cup raw shrimp (deveined)
1 pkg. kielbasa sausage (chopped)
1 (8 oz.) pkg. sweet-mini peppers (finely chopped)
1 cup sundried tomatoes (finely chopped)
2 quarts of chicken stock
1 cup light or heavy cream
1 cup onion
3 garlic cloves
1 cup fresh parsley (dry is fine as well)
¼ cup Worcestershire sauce
2 cups water
1 tsp. creole seasonings
½ tsp. black pepper
½ tsp. salt
½ tsp. garlic powder
4 tbsps. canola oil

Roux:

½ cup flour
1 tsp. turmeric
2 tbsp. canola oil

Preheat large pot with canola oil.

Step 1: In a large mixing bowl, season the chicken with salt, pepper, creole seasoning, and garlic powder. Place chicken in pot and seer for 5 minutes on each side or until its browned on both sides. Remove chicken from pot and set aside.

Step 2: For the roux, leave the pot on stovetop, add flour and turmeric. Stir roux for approximately 8 to 10 minutes. Once the roux has darkened to a golden yellow, remove pot from stovetop and cool for 20 minutes.

Step 3: After the roux has cooled, return pot to stovetop and add 2 more tablespoon of oil. Add sundried tomatoes, sweet mini peppers, onions, and garlic; sauté until translucent. Add Worcestershire sauce and stir roux for 3 minutes.

Step 4: To the pot, stir in chicken stock, heavy cream, and water until combined. Return the chicken and add kielbasa to the pot and bring to a boil, reduce the heat, and simmer uncovered for 45 minutes.

Step 5: Add shrimp and parsley the last 5 minutes of cooking time. Ladle up and serve over rice or favorite pasta. Make 4 to 6 servings.

Cooking Advisory Tip: This is a good soup to keep you warm while you are listening to the birds singing at sunrise.

"Fishing King" Cacciatore

The word "cacciatore" in Italian cuisine means "hunter." For me, growing up in an isolated rural area, where the deer and woods were my neighbors, to hunt meant, there was going to be a lot of stalking in late fall by an unknown "shooter" lurking somewhere in the woods. It was scary word, if it did not personally benefit your empty stomach.

Although I never hunt down anything other than a plate of food, the word hunt for me brings back memories of when I would tag along with my father to go fishing. He would start early in the morning and leave just before the deer came out the woods to summons him to leave the premises. Other than being there to guard the fish, and to remind my father of the deliciousness of those fishes between some "hot" buttered hoe cakes–my father did most of all the work to convince another fish to go home with us. As a matter of fact, when I would remind my father it was time to depart the pond, he would say, "In a minute, I'm waiting for another bite." As a five year old kid, I'm thinking, "I don't want another fish to take home, I just wanted the fishes that were ready to go home."

As I became an adult, I eventually began to understand how my father's faith kept his families' stomach from being empty. He carried the burden for taking care of his seeds. He stayed the course, he did not leave us, and he stayed until he joined my mother in heaven. He was my role model of what a man is planted on this earth to be. There will never be another hunter like my father–he will always be my "Fishing King."

Ingredients

3 pieces cod fish
1 lb. devein shrimp (Medium–43/50)
2 cups dice tomatoes w/ basil, garlic, & oregano
1 cup Pinot Grigio wine
¼ cup flour
1 ½ tbsp. heavy or light cream
2 tbsps. tarragon (chopped)
2 garlic cloves (minced)
¼ cup onions
1 tsp. red pepper flakes
1 Bay leaf
6 tbsps. unsalted butter (reserve 2 tbsp.)
2 tsps. sugar
2 tsps. salt (reserve 1 tsp.)
½ tsp. onion powder
½ lemon wedge
2 tsps. canola oil (reserve 1 tsp.)

Preheat deep skillet with 1 tsp. of oil and reserve butter.

Step 1: In a mixing bowl, whisk together flour and salt. Add shrimp to bowl and massage flour into shrimp. Place shrimp in preheated skillet and sauté for 1 second on each side. Remove from skillet and transfer to a plate with paper towel to remove excess oil. Set aside.

Step 2: In the same skillet, add butter and oil. Sauté cod for 2 minutes–squeezing lemon juice on each side of fish while searing. Remove cod from pan and set aside. Add onions, garlic, tarragon, and red pepper flakes to skillet. Sauté until vegetables are translucent. Add wine, tomatoes, cream, onion powder, sugar, and bay leaf. Cook for 12 to 15 minutes until sauce thickens. Place cod back into pan and simmer for 15 minutes.

Step 3: Add shrimp the last 10 minutes of cooking time and cook for an additional 5 minutes. Remove bay leaf and serve with some toasted garlic bread and enjoy. Make 4 servings.

Cooking Advisory Tip: Even if you are not a fisherman, take time out of your busy schedule to adventure out with your children. Remember, "When you take the time to be an active parent during your children's formative years, they will return that same quality time to you, during your elderly years."

JERK JAMBALAYA

If you enjoy travelling, but don't have time to plan a vacation because you are too consumed with locking down a potential love mate, why not bring the cuisine from your dream destination right to your kitchen. May I suggest a taste of Jamaica and New Orleans to spice up your high speed pursuit? These two genres of food will give you more than enough spice to kick up your "stay home" vacation in style.

INGREDIENTS

1 lb. kielbasa sausage
1 ½ lb. medium shrimp (peeled & deveined
¼ cup tomato paste
1 (32 oz.) container vegetable stock
2 ½ cups rice
1 cup onions
1 cup scallions
3 garlic cloves
1 tbsp. fresh ginger
1 habanero chili pepper (optional)
½ cup fresh thyme
2 bay leaves
1 cup water
1 tsp. cinnamon
1 tsp. cumin
1 tsp nutmeg
½ tsp allspice
1 tsp. kosher salt
1 tsp. black pepper

1 ½ tsp. sugar
1 tbsp. canola oil
½ cup fresh parsley (garnish)

Preheat a large pot or Dutch oven with oil.

Step 1: Sauté sausage, onions, scallions, garlic, cinnamon, cumin, nutmeg, allspice, salt, black pepper, and sugar for 5 minutes.

Step 2: Add tomato paste, stock, water, chili pepper, ginger, bay leaf and thyme, and stir ingredients. Bring mixture to a boil for 5 minutes. Cover, reduce heat, and simmer for 25 minutes.

Step 3: Add shrimp the last 5 minutes of cooking time. Add rice to pot and cook rice according time specified on package. Garnish with parsley and enjoy. Make 4 to 6 servings.

Cooking Advisory Tip: If you are not into spicy food or a spicy love life, please remove the habanero chili pepper from this recipe.

A "Real" Veggie Burger

Most of veggie burgers that I have examined in my lifetime seemed to have been developed from some kind of concoction that was compressed together to look like a rock. For me, in order to be an authentic veggie burger, you should be able to identify the actual vegetables and meat that is incorporated into the patty. In short, if a veggie burger is not properly prepared, it can either tarnish a Home Cook's reputation, or make them walk around in shame.

If you have been eating a veggie burger that is unidentifiable for a Crime Scene Investigator (CSI) to dissect, you should slowly put the burger back on the plate, walk away from the table, and call the local authorities to lock it up! Once you have executed this task, take the time and go into your kitchen to make, "A "Real" Veggie Burger."

Ground Meat

1 lb. ground beef (93% lean & 7% fat) or ground chicken

Veggies for Meat

1 cup carrots
2 radishes
½ jalapeno pepper (seeds out)
1 tbsp. sundried tomatoes
3 parsley sprigs (fresh)
¼ tsp. chipotle juice
1 ¼ tsp. salt

1 tsp. black pepper
1 tsp. cumin
3 tsps. olive or canola oil

Topping for Burger

1 ½ cup yellow squash
¾ cup sliced baby bella mushrooms
¾ cup onions
¾ cup green bell pepper
1 ¼ tbsp. canola oil
2 tbsps. margarine

Vegetable Mixture: In a food processor, pulse carrots, radishes, fresh parsley, jalapeno pepper, sundried tomatoes, chipotle juice, salt, black pepper, and cumin. Slowly add oil to vegetables. Pour mixture into a medium bowl and set aside.

Preheat large non-stick pan with oil.

Meat: In a mixing bowl, incorporate the vegetable mixture into ground meat. Form 4 hamburger patties; cook burgers for 10 or 12 minutes on each side. Once burger is cooked to your preference, remove burgers from pan and place on a plate with paper towel to remove excess oil.

Topping: Using the same pan, clean out access oil with a paper towel. Add canola oil and margarine. Add squash, onions, and green pepper, sauté until translucent. Add the mushrooms and cook for additional 5 minutes until all veggies are caramelized. Add salt or black pepper if desired.

Assembly: Toast a burger bun and add burger topped with vegetable mixture. Make 4 servings.

Cooking Advisory Tip: When eating this burger, hold it tight, and have plenty of napkins to catch the juices. Also, after eating this burger, you should have gotten most of the recommended daily allowance of vegetables.

Shrimp & Turf Burger

Have you ever gone to a five-star restaurant and the menu item for surf and turf had the words "Market Price (MP)" written beside it? If so, I hope your waiter was kind of enough to give you a crash course in food economics. In short, the price of your meal can be set by the restaurateur to pay off any debt that he or she has lingering out there. There are no limitations for a MP. It could end up costing a patron the following:

1. Five grocery bag lunches for a kindergartner with a big appetite;
2. Fifty full course meals at Grandma's house; and
3. Labor cost to harvest 5,000 sacks of potatoes.

If you feel any of these scenarios are applicable to you, there is still time to flee the restaurant before the bills comes. When you leave, hold your head up, and walk out with some swagger. Be proud of yourself for managing to get out of there–before you were recognized as the "Meat Grease Food Critic (MGFC)." I don't think they would have taken too kindly to you leaving a "grease stain" on their perfectly white table cloth.

Ingredients

1 lb. ground beef (93% lean & 7% fat)
10 large shrimp (rough chopped)
2 cups shredded gouda cheese
1 ¼ cup milk
1 tbsp. butter or margarine
1 tbsp. garlic powder

1 tsp. salt
1 tsp. black pepper
2 tbsps. canola oil

Preheat medium size nonstick pan with oil.

Burger: In a large mixing bowl, mix ground meat with garlic powder, salt, and black pepper. Place the patties in pan and cook for approximately 10 minutes on each side. Remove burgers from pan and transfer to a plate with paper a towel to remove access oil. Set aside.

Shrimp: In same pan, wipe out with a paper towel. Add butter or margarine to clean sauce pan. Add shrimp and cook for 1 minute. Add cheese and milk, cook until cheese is dissolved. Pour shrimp sauce over burger and throw down like it's no bodies business! Make 4 servings.

Cooking Advisory Tip: This recipe is for the Home Cook who wants to make a surf and turf meal that's really below market price.

Asian Soul Stir Fry

When cooking became a hobby for me, I wanted to experiment with all genres of foods. If I had to call it, I would say, Asian cuisine was somewhat a challenge for me. Like any other genre of foods, if you know the basics ingredients of a culture, the dish can be successfully executed if you are willing to put some "soul" into it. This key component will make it effortless. Once a Home Cook realizes this, he or she will have the confidence to "pimp" down a high-class fashion show–in their bare feet!

Ingredients

½ roll "hot" ground sausage
¾ pkg. of spaghetti
1 whole small cabbage
½ cup carrots
1 (8 oz.) pkg. baby bella mushrooms
½ red bell pepper
2 garlic cloves
1 tsp. ginger

Sauce

¼ cup of low sodium soy sauce
2 ½ tsps. corn starch
1 tsp. raw sugar
½ cup of orange marmalade
1 tsp. sriracha (optional)
3 tbsps. water

Step 1: In a large pot, boil spaghetti according to box instructions. Drain in a colander and set aside.

Step 2: Preheat a wok or deep nonstick pan. Add sausage and cook until brown. Remove sausage from pan and place on paper towel to remove access grease. Pour ½ of the oil in pan, into a grease can. Add garlic, ginger, mushrooms, bell pepper, carrots, and cabbage. Cook vegetables until translucent. Transport sausage and spaghetti back into the pan, cook for 12 minutes.

Step 3: In a mixing bowl, mix soy sauce, sugar, sriracha, corn starch, water, and orange marmalade. Pour sauce over stir fry. Cook for an additional 5 minutes. Plate up and enjoy. Make 4 to 6 servings.

Cooking Advisory Tip: Whenever cooking this stir fry, you can switch out the sausage with chicken or ham. There are no limitations when cooking Asian soul.

CHEESELESS LASAGNA

What if you woke up one morning, and there was a News report that cows were no longer producing milk? Would you accept it, or would you stalk a first-time Mother who was not aware of the milk shortage? Whatever you might be plotting, you will have to come to terms with the fact, that in life, nothing is guaranteed forever–not even the milk from a "worn out" cow. If you want to prepare for this possible catastrophe, get a head start, and cook some "Cheeseless Lasagna," who knows, you might realize there's more than one way to milk a recipe.

MEAT SAUCE

    1 (12 oz.) box oven ready lasagna
    3 lbs. ground chicken
    1 cup roasted bell peppers
    4 garlic cloves
    2 (28 oz.) can crushed tomatoes w/ basil, garlic, and oregano
    1 tsp. salt
    1 tsp. black pepper
    1 tsp. garlic powder
    3 tbsps. agave nectar
    1 tbsp. Worchester sauce
    3 tbsps. vegetable oil

Preheat oven to 375° degrees.

Zucchini/Corn Sauce:

> 2 ½ cups zucchini (finely diced)
> 1 (14.5 oz.) can sweet corn (cream style)
> 4 garlic cloves
> 1 large onion
> 1 tbsp. fresh basil
> 1 tsp. salt
> 1 tsp. black pepper
> 3 tbsps. vegetable oil

Step 1: For the lasagna, cook according to box instructions and set aside.

Step 2: In a medium size pan, add vegetable oil. Add zucchini, onions, corn, garlic, salt, and pepper; cook for 5 minutes. After vegetables are cooked, pour them into a blender or food processor and add the basil. Puree until smooth and set aside.

Meat Sauce: In a large pot, add vegetable oil and sauté garlic, roasted pepper, salt and pepper, cook until translucent. Add ground chicken and break apart with a wooden spoon. Add crush tomatoes, garlic powder, worchester sauce, and agave. Cook meat sauce for 25 to 30 minutes or until sauce has thickened.

Layering the Lasagna: Spray casserole dish with nonstick spray; begin the 1st layer with meat sauce, lasagna, and zucchini/corn sauce. Repeat steps with the last layer of lasagna topped with meat sauce. Cover casserole dish with foil and bake for 50 minutes. Remove foil the last 10 minutes of cooking time. Remove lasagna from oven and allow it to cool for 15 minutes before serving. Make 8 to 10 servings.

Cooking Advisory Tip: If you want to add cheese to this lasagna, feel free to do so. This recipe was created from the guilt that I felt for creating that high cholesterol "Witness Protection Program (WPP) Meat Sauce," in Chapter 2, of this comedic cookbook. Please, "I beg for your pardon!"

Ham Shrimp Mac & Cheese

There should not be a person on this earth who does not look forward to a delicious casserole dish of macaroni and cheese—it's the "matriarch" of all comfort foods. The cheese alone will not only bring all the ingredients together, it will give an introverted Home Cook the reassurance they can cook cheese without burning it up. After this discovery, the Home Cook will be able to bring world peace between a radical politician and his mother–if they are not afraid of mixing the cheese with the macaroni noodles.

Ingredients

1 pound devein shrimp (chopped)
2 cups dice ham
1 (16 oz.) box elbow or corkscrew pasta
1 (12 oz.) pkg. smoke gouda cheese (diced)
1 cup white cheddar cheese (diced)
¾ cup wheat bread
½ cup saltine crackers
½ cup all-purpose white whole wheat flour
6 tbsps. butter (reserve 3 tbsp.)
2 cups whole milk
½ cup light cream
½ cup pasta water (reserve)
½ tsp. old bay seasoning
¼ tsp. course black pepper
¼ tsp. kosher salt
Nonstick spray

Preheat oven to 350° degrees.

Pasta: Bring water to a boil and add salt, cook pasta according to package instructions. Drain pasta and pour in a large mixing bowl and set aside.

Meats: In small sauce pan, melt butter and sautéed ham and shrimp for 1 minute. Add black pepper and old bay seasoning, transfer into a small bowl, and set aside.

Cheese Sauce: In a large pot or Dutch oven, melt butter. Sprinkle flour over butter and stir roux until thicken. Gradually add the milk and cream. Add smoke gouda and white cheddar cheese (add pasta water to loosen the sauce if needed). Fold in ham and shrimp and pour cheese sauce over pasta and thoroughly mix. Spray a 9X13 casserole dish with nonstick spray. Transfer mac and cheese into casserole dish and set aside.

Bread Crumbs: With a food processor, pulse bread and crackers together. Sprinkle topping over mac and cheese. Place casserole dish in oven and bake for 30 minutes. Remove from oven and cool for 30 minutes before indulging. Make 10 to 12 servings.

Note: If you want the top of the mac and cheese to be "browner," place casserole dish under the broiler for 1 minute or until you have achieved the preferred brownness.

Cooking Advisory Tip: If you are a vegetarian and you would prefer this mac and cheese to be meatless, feel free to dismiss the ham and shrimp–see how thoughtful I am.

Prenuptial Potato Salad

As a child, my mother would make potato salad every Sunday. For the longest time, I could not understand why my mother preferred to utilize her hands peeling a bushel of potatoes, rather than calming me down from my screaming tan chums. I just assumed peeling potatoes was more important than me–at least that what I thought.

It was not until years later, my mother revealed to me, the real reason there was always a sack of potatoes on the back porch. Apparently, my mother and father had this agreement that potato salad would be prepared every Sunday for the duration of their marriage. I guess one would say they had a "Food Prenup (FP)," which simply means, a Home Cook who is mandated to cook a specific meal, on a specified day, to keep the marriage blissful. Apparently, my father had a contingency in that agreement as well, to give my mother enough children to work those fields to retrieve those potatoes. I only wish my parents would have shared this critical information with me and my siblings. Maybe we would have had some leverage over them to notify Child Protective Services (CPS), for working us in those fields during the time there were "heat" advisories warnings. Maybe we still might have a chance in getting some kind of restitution from our parents for:

* Instilling faith and good work ethics to protect us against people who might not like a rooted potato;
* Strengthening our managing abilities for a CEO position at big time potato corporation; and
* Giving us wisdom to determine the intentions of a manipulative potato head that flaunts "waving money" in hopes we would compromise our integrity.

The life lesson for this story was more than a married couple using potato salad as a contingency for their union. It was about how two people plotted, early in their marriage, on how to produce enough children, to "dig" a potato–for a bowl of potato salad. I tell you, "Parents can do some cruel things to their children!"

INGREDIENTS

4 cups potato (diced yukon gold)
2 boiled eggs (diced)
¾ cup sandwich spread
5 chive springs (chopped)
1 mini red sweet pepper (finely chopped)
2 tbsps. sweet pickle relish
2 tbsps. yellow mustard
1 tsp. paprika
1 tbsp. sugar
½ tsp. salt

Step 1: Cut potatoes in quarter cubes and place in a pot of cold water. Bring potatoes to a boil and cook for 20 minutes. Drain the water off and transfer potatoes into a large mixing bowl.

Step 2: Add eggs, chives, sweet pepper, pickle relish, mustard, sugar, salt, and sandwich spread. Mix together with hands until all ingredients are well incorporated. Garnish with paprika and refrigerate. Make 4 to 6 servings.

Cooking Advisory Tip: A food commitment is the key to keeping down the divorce rate, and keeping others from digging into your marital affairs. Please make a food commitment today–it's never too late.

Mediterranean Creamy Chicken & Spinach Pasta

If you are a Home Cook with an intense pilot for good food, you might attempt to utilize your kitchen more often. This new experience will allow you to leave your comfort zone, to prepare a different genre of food that your spouse will probably not enjoy. Don't fret, he just wants the meals that he is accustom to. Remember, move slow, breath out, and don't allow him to distract you from creating a delicious meal that he's eventually going to eat anyway.

Ingredients

1 lb. chicken tenderloin (cut into ¼ bite sizes
1 (8 oz.) cream cheese w/ bacon
½ box multi grain pasta
4 cups fresh spinach
¼ cup Spanish olives (chopped)
4 mini sweet peppers (finely chopped)
1 medium onion
3 garlic cloves
3 tbsps. canola oil or olive oil

Chicken Seasoning

½ tsp. garlic powder
¼ tsp. cumin
½ tsp. turmeric
¼ tsp. cayenne pepper

1 tsp. oregano
½ tsp. salt
½ tsp. black pepper

Step 1: Season chicken with dry spices (garlic powder, cumin, turmeric, salt, black/cayenne pepper and oregano). Marinate chicken overnight for more of an intense flavor. Remove from refrigerator. Allow chicken to come to room temperature for 30 minutes before cooking.

Step 2: Boil pasta according to box instructions. After pasta has finish cooking, drain water and reserve 1 cup of pasta water. Set aside.

Step 3: Preheat a large sauce pan with oil. Add onions, peppers, olives, and garlic; sauté until translucent. Add the chicken to pan and fully cook. Add the spinach and cook until withered. Add cream cheese and cook for 10 minutes. Fold in pasta and basil 5 minutes at the end of cooking time. Make 4 to 6 servings.

Cooking Advisory Tip: This meal is right tasty–you will definitely need to pull back from the table to decrease your chances from sinning.

CHAPTER 8

A Taste & Something Sweet: Tasty desserts "The Righteous Drinker (TRD)" will keep consuming.

• • •

A One Roll, Jelly Roll

In life, no two people will execute the same task the same way. One person will master the technique without any issues, whereas the other person will make an error–at least that's their mind set. Sometimes an error is just a new discovery, working in your favor.

The standard jelly roll is rolled at least three times. For me, in attempting to roll over a flatten piece of cake two times, while keeping the jelly intact, was a bit challenging. You could have good intentions but sometimes the objective is not achievable. If you are like me and other "sweaty" Home Cooks before us, they probably found it easier to wrestle an alligator coated with meat grease, than to roll over a flatten piece of cake. It's embarrassing for a Home Cook to explain to others why a cake won't roll over. If you can only get one roll from that cake, without breaking it, than you have done your part. Be true to yourself and stop trying to please everybody. It could make you look like you are trying to hide something, or that you are the only Home Cook out there with a unique looking jelly roll.

If there was a moral to this story, it would be, "If you are able to get one roll, out of a jelly roll, than no one should question your decision to name your recipe, "A One Roll, Jelly Roll."

Ingredients

Preheat oven to 350° degrees.

    1 box Yellow Cake Mix (bake according to box directions)
    1 ½ cup grape jelly
    3 eggs

1 cup water
1/3 cup vegetable oil

1 pkg. cream cheese (room temperature)
½ cup confectionary sugar
1 tsp. vanilla extract

Preheat oven to 350° degrees.

Cake: In a large mixing bowl, mix cake ingredients and follow cake box instructions. Once cake batter has been mixed, place parchment paper on a sheet pan. Spread cake batter evening on sheet pan. If there are air bubbles, pick pan up and gently drop unto counter without spilling batter on the floor. Place cake in oven and bake according to box instructions. Once the cake is baked, allow it to cool for approximately 45 minutes. Spread grape jelly on ½ of the cake. Slowly roll the cake 1 time, and place in the serving plate.

Icing: In a medium bowl, use an electric hand mixer to beat the cream cheese and vanilla. Gradually incorporate confectionary sugar into cream cheese until it becomes smooth.

Icing the entire roll and be proud of a new way of making a jelly roll. Make 6 to 8 servings.

Cooking Advisory Tip: This recipe is dedicated to the baker out there, who wants to turn their recipe flaws into something unique.

Lay Off the Coconut Rum Pie

Every now and then, everybody has taken a "taste," which is merely taking a sip or two of liquor. If you are a "Tastee," you have probably elevated from a jar of moonshine to top shelf liquor.

Other than a "Tastee," there is another type of sipper out there called, "The Righteous Drinker (TRD)," you know these people very well. They are the ones who swear up and down they never had a taste a day in their lives. It's just this type of unrevealing confession that makes you want hire a Private Investigator (PI) to ransack their kitchen. Believe me, if a TRD is a baker, they have been a tasting for a very long time–they just don't want to admit their hitting those flavored extracts. If you don't believe me, the next time you visit a TRD's house, take a peek in their pantry. I bet you, there's enough flavored extracts to produce a liquor distribution center. Yes, flavored extracts could have as much as 90%, and as little as 17% of alcohol in a two fluid ounce bottle. Don't be shocked, now you know why Grandma wasn't hollering at the kids when she was baking. She was preoccupied with "tasting" the cake batter to make sure the extract was–all up in it!

Do me a favor, the next time a TRD declares they have NEVER taken a taste, give them a slice of this pie. Make sure you have a hidden camera to capture the indulgence. Other than an unexpected trip to Emergency Room (ER), or realizing that photography is really not your forte, "What's the worst that can happen from taking my shady advice?" I don't see it causing any more physical harm.

Ingredients

1 ½ cup coconut flakes
3 tbsps. all-purpose flour

¼ cup coconut rum

2 tsp. coconut extracts (reserve 1 tbsp. for custard)

1 cup light cream

5 eggs (beaten)

1 cup sugar

3 tbsps. butter (melted)

1 (9-inch) unbaked pie shell

Preheat oven to 400° degrees.

Step 1: Allow crust to thaw for 10-20 minutes. Prick the bottom and side of crust with fork. Bake crust in oven for 11-14 minutes. Cool and set aside.

Step 2: In a small mixing bowl, add coconut rum and extract and whisk together. Fold in coconut flakes and allow it to marinate in liquids for 15 minutes.

Step 3: In a large mixing bowl, whisk together butter, flour, eggs, sugar, extract, and cream. Fold custard into the coconut mixture. Pour custard into pie shell and bake for 55 to 60 minutes. Remove from oven and allow pie to cool for 10 minutes (overnight in refrigerator makes it firmer). Make 6 servings.

Cooking Advisory Tip: If you are under 25 years of age, you are still too young to eat this pie. Commit your time to ensuring Grandma is not driving or tripping over the furniture.

Margarita Key Lime Cheesecake

If you enjoy a tasty margarita drink and key lime pie, you should marry these two indulgences into one. Imagine how a key lime pie with a heavy hand of Tequila would taste. Well, you don't have to imagine no more, I have executed such a desert. Just know, for this recipe, the reduction of Tequila usage was purposely altered for safety purposes. Trust me, "No one should be alone with a hot cake in the oven, and a bottle of Tequila!"

Crust

1 box Graham crackers (27 crackers)
½ cup oats
½ cup brown sugar
1 ¾ stick of butter (melted)

Preheat oven to 350° degrees.

Step 1: In small batches, pulse crackers and sugar in food processor until complete. Transfer crackers to a large bowl. Pulse the oaks in food processor and transfer to bowl. Whisk ingredients together. Pour melted butter over cracker mixture and stir until incorporated. Once butter is well distributed, the graham cracker crumbs will began to stick together.

Pour cracker crumbs into a 10-inch spring form pan and press with a measuring cup on the bottom and sides of pan. Place in oven and bake for 12 to 15 minutes. Remove crust from oven and cool for 1 hour before adding the cheese cake filling.

CHEESE CAKE FILLING

1 (8 oz.) cream cheese (room temperature)
1 cup crush pineapple
1 (14 oz.) can sweeten condense milk
6 egg whites (reserve 2 egg yolks)
2 limes zested
¾ cup key lime juice

Maintain preheated oven at 350° degrees.

Step 2: In large mixing bowl, use hand or cake mixer to mix cream cheese, condense milk, and egg whites. To the batter, add egg yolk, one at a time, and gradually add the key lime juice. Fold in pineapple and lime zest. Pour mixture into the prepared graham cracker crust. Place pan unto a sheet pan with a rack in oven (pour water into bottom of sheet pan to keep the cheesecake filling moist). Bake for 40 minutes in oven. Remove cheese cake filling from oven and cool for 20 minutes.

CAKE

1 Yellow box cake
2 (12 oz.) containers cream cheese icing
1 pkg. lime gelatin
¼ cup orange juice
¼ cup margarita (4 squeezed limes, 4 tbsp. agave & 2 ½ tbsp. Tequila)
3 large eggs

1 cup water
1/3 vegetable oil

Maintain preheated oven at 350° degrees.

Step 3: In large mixing bowl, stir cake mix and gelatin until incorporated. Add eggs, oil, water, orange juice, and mix with a hand mixer. Spray baking pan with nonstick spray or line with parchment paper and pour batter into 10 by 2-inch round pan. Bake 33-36 minutes and set aside.

Step 4: Once "cake" is removed from oven and still hot, place holes throughout the cake. Generously base the cake with ¼ of the margarita mixture. Allow cake to cool before icing.

Step 5: Place "cake" over the prepared "cheesecake filling" and icing the cake only. Place the cake in refrigerator to set-up for 30 minutes before slicing. Serve 10 to 12 people.

Cooking Advisory Tip: If you only have one 10 inch spring form pan because you are too cheap to purchase a 10 by 2-inch round pan, this MKLC will take two days to prepare. If you want the cake and cheesecake assembly to be accurate, it's really in your best interest to purchase another 10 by 2-inch round pan before you start sipping on the margarita mixture. Remember, don't drink, drive, or drink tequila while baking this cheesecake. You need to focus your attention on trying to follow these drawn-out instructions for this recipe.

Low-Down Dirty Devil Food Cheesecake

Back in the day, it was not unusual to hear folks say, "You just low down and dirty!" It was not a nice thing to say to someone who was already questioning their personal hygiene decisions. If you were that individual, try not to allow those comments to become embedded in your head–whereas you really believe you are a low down and dirty individual. Instead, occupy your time with preparing this recipe to demonstrate to those malicious people–you really are a clean person.

Crust

> 1 (14.4 oz.) box chocolate graham crackers (finely chopped)
> 1 stick butter or margarine (melted)
> 1 cup toasted coconut flakes
> 1 cup oats

Preheat oven to 350° degrees.

Step 1: In food processor, pulse graham crackers and oats. Transfer crackers to a large bowl and add coconut flakes and melted margarine. Mix ingredients together and pour into a 10 inch springform pan. Press graham cracker crumbs into the bottom and side of pan with a measuring cup. Place in oven and bake crust for 12 to 15 minutes. Remove crust from oven and cool for 1 hour before adding the cheese cake filling.

CHEESE FILLING

2 (8 oz.) cream cheese (room temperature)
2 tbsps. all-purpose flour (sifted)
¼ cup sugar
1 tsp. rum extract
4 large eggs plus 2 egg yolks (room temperature)

Step 2: Beat cream cheese with hand mixer. Fold in sugar, flour, and rum extract. Add eggs and beat 1 at a time until it's incorporated into filling. Set aside.

CAKE BATTER (BOX CAKE IS FINE AS WELL)

1½ cup cake flour
1 cup cocoa powder
2 eggs (room temperature)
1 ¼ cup sugar
1 tsp. baking soda
1 tsp. of baking powder
½ tsp. salt
1 cup milk
2 tsps. coconut extract
1 cup vegetable oil

Cake Batter: Combine flour, cocoa, sugar, baking soda, baking powder, and salt. With a hand or cake mixer, beat ingredients until well incorporated. Add eggs, milk, oil, and rum extract, beat on medium speed for 2 minutes and set aside.

<u>Assembling</u>: Preheat oven to 325° degrees.

Step 1: Place sheet pan with a rack in oven, and pour water into pan. Place in oven.

Step 2: In the springform pan with prepared crust pour: (1) 1 inch of cake batter over crust; 2) pour 1 inch of crème cheese mixture, and 3) pour 1 inch of the cake batter. Take a fork or toothpick to create the marvel effect on top of the cake.

Step 3: Bake for 1 hour and 15 minutes or until center is set (test the middle of cake 45 minutes of cooking time with a toothpick). Take out of oven and cool on wire rack. Refrigerate 4 hours or overnight. Serve 10 to 12 people.

Cooking Advisory Tip: This is a good desert to make to test your patience level. When you pass this test, try testing your patience with removing a car engine and placing it back into the car within 1 day–this act will make you grateful that you tackled this recipe versus a car engine.

Mistaken Macaroon S'more Cookies

Have you ever had a creative thought that you wanted to execute in a specific way, but it went another way? Like braiding and setting your Maltese's hair on rollers so he could become a Bishon Frise. That would be considered a "bad creative thought," that turn out to be bad hair day for your Maltese.

Sometimes a mistake can turn out to be great invention–or a costly divorce. Taking risks, is not all bad, it just alerts one's brain cells there is a hostile takeover occurring and ideas are being conformed in a different way. This would be the case of my original plan for creating a "Graham Cracker Macaroon S'more," for a campfire dessert.

At first, the formation of the ball was intact until it was placed in the oven–the heat caused the ball to flatten into a cookie. Although that unexpected mistake occurred, everything worked out for the best. I'm sure glad it did, because I was plotting on how to convince the Grocery Store Manager that the ingredients for this recipe was outdated, so I could receive a refund for the "mishap" ingredients. A move like that, would have made me a shady and cheap person–it's always best to be a person with integrity.

Ingredients

1 cup graham crackers
2 cups sweetened shredded coconut (1 cup for toasting & 1 reserve cup)
½ cup marshmallow fluff (keep chilled until use)
½ cup sweeten condense milk
3 egg whites
½ tsp. coconut extract

Preheat oven 350° degrees.

Step 1: Heat a nonstick pan to toast coconut flakes. Stir for approximately 4 minutes or until lightly brown. Remove from pan and pour coconut flakes into mixing bowl. Set aside to cool.

Step 2: Coconut/Cracker Mixture: With a food processor or ziploc bag, finely chop up graham crackers. Transfer cracker mixture to the mixing bowl of toasted coconut flakes. Add coconut extract and mix well. Set aside.

Step 3: Fluff Mixture: In a separate mixing bowl, mix fluff, condense milk, and eggs. Once mix is well incorporated, fold fluff mixture into cracker and coconut mixture. Use a ¾ diameter ice cream scooper to scoop batter. Once batter is scooped, roll each ball in the reserve toasted coconut. Place on a sheet pan lined with parchment paper and bake for 15 to 18 minutes. Remove from oven and cool. Make 12 dozen.

CHOCOLATE SAUCE

> ½ cup white chocolate morsels
> ½ cup bittersweet chocolate baking morsel or chips
> 1 tbsp. coconut rum
> 2 tbsps. margarine or butter
> 4 cups of water (reserve 1 tbsp. of the hot water)

Step 4: Add water to sauce pan and bring to a boil. Place a mixing bowl over boiling water. Add butter and stir morsels until melted. Remove bowl from sauce pan, add rum and little water to loosen the sauce and cool for 5 minutes. Transfer sauce into a nozzle bottle and drizzle chocolate over cookies.

Cooking Advisory Tip: These soft delicious cookies can still be used at your next outdoor outing. Just insert your favorite chocolate bar between two of these cookies, wrap with foil, and roast over a campfire.

CARROT & SWEET POTATO BOURBON BREAD PUDDING

If you like bread pudding and a taste, you will love this "Carrot and Sweet Potato Bourbon Bread Pudding." This recipe will give you the beta-carotene you need, and a reason to go the liquor store for a justifiable cause. Once you are prepared to make this bread pudding, please make sure you are not "sipping" the bourbon sauce when preparing it. You will need every bit of it to saturate each serving of the bread pudding. Be mindful, if you prefer to eliminate the liquor from this recipe, I must warn you, the bread pudding will lose its deliciousness. If you are planning on using all the bourbon for the sauce, you should do the following:

* Inform your "ailing" guests the exact amount of bourbon that's in the bourbon sauce—they will need to know this information in case they need a miraculous recovery from their illness;
* Alert your neighbors in advance that they will be serving as designated drivers for your guest and possibly you; and
* Lock all interior doors to the house for the self-righteous guests, who were too "uppity" to indulge in this delicious bread pudding. Keep your eye on them. They have been patiently waiting all evening, for everyone to start feeling extra nice–so they could rob your house!

CUSTARD & BREAD MIXTURE

1 French baguette
1 cup crush pineapple (drain the juice)
1 ½ cup light cream

½ cup milk
¼ cup brown sugar
4 egg yolks (beaten)
1 tbsp. bourbon
1 tsp. vanilla (rum is good also) extract
pinch of salt

Preheat oven at 350° degrees.

Step 1: Cut baguette into ¼ quarter pieces. Spread out on a sheet pan and bake in the oven for 15 minutes. Remove toasted bread from oven and set aside.

Step 2: In a large mixing bowl, combine pineapple, cream, milk, brown sugar, egg yolks, bourbon, vanilla and salt. Add the toasted bread and marinate for 30 minutes.

CARROTS & SWEET POTATO MIXTURE

¼ cup brown sugar & cinnamon cream cheese
½ cup sweet potato (precooked)
½ cup carrots (finely chop in Food Processor)
1 egg
½ tsp. vanilla extract
1 tbsp. butter (melted)
1 ¼ cup brown sugar
¼ tsp. cinnamon
¼ tsp. nutmeg

Step 3: In mixing bowl, use a hand mixer to mix cream cheese, sweet potato, carrots, egg, extract, butter, brown sugar, cinnamon, and nutmeg. Once thoroughly mix, fold carrot and sweet potato mixture into prepared custard and bread mixture.

Step 4: Pour half of bread pudding into a 9X13 casserole dish. Sprinkle raisins on the first layer, add the remaining mixture bread pudding and add more raisins to garnish the top. Cover bread pudding with foil and bake for 45 minutes.

TOPPING

    3 tbsps. unsalted butter (cut into cubes)
    3 tbsps. sugar
    ½ tsp. cinnamon

Step 5: In a small mixing bowl, mix butter, sugar, and cinnamon. Take bread pudding out of oven after 45 minutes of cooking time and sprinkle topping over BP. Place BP back in oven "uncovered" for additional 20 to 25 minutes so the BP will be crisp.

Note: For extra crispness, place BP under the broiler and monitor it so it won't burn up.

BOURBON SAUCE

    ¾ cup light or heavy cream
    2 tbsps. sugar
    ½ tsp. corn starch
    ¼ cup bourbon
    Pinch of salt
    2 tsps. butter

In a mixing bowl, mix corn starch and bourbon to make a "slurry." Pour slurry in a small sauce pan and place on stovetop. Whisk in the cream, sugar, salt, and butter. Allow sauce to thicken. Once sauce has thickened, remove from heat and pour over individual slices of BP. Make 8 to 10 servings.

Cooking Advisory Tip: If you plan on taking this BP for lunch, adhere to your employers' "No Drinking" policy. It's probably best that you take this BP to your next holiday party, since that's when your colleagues are at their happiest!

Jungle Woman Fruit Pie

For the duration of my high school years, I was known as "Jungle Woman." It was a name that I rightfully claimed and still honor. I wouldn't say I was a menace in school, just a little bit untamed. For some reason, the Principal never took any disciplinary actions against me. That was partially because he knew my father would not have taken too kindly to him disciplining his baby girl–for an action he could not prove.

As age has come upon me, I had to allow the Jungle Woman to settle down inside me. Although there are times I do want to bring her back to let loose on my supervisor, I realize that she should remain dormant until there's a real need for her to come forth. The only time that would occur, if there's a class reunion with my classmates. They are the only ones who truly knew how to bring a Jungle Woman's "holla" out of me.

For me, going to school was more than just socializing all day long, it was some of the best adventures of my childhood. This recipe is dedicated to my classmates, the extended family that will always be a part of my jungle.

Cool Whip Mixture

2 (8 oz.) container cool whip
1 tbsp. lemon juice
½ can condense milk
1 (8 oz.) can crush pineapples (drain)
1 cup fresh white or yellow peaches (diced)
1 cup of fresh strawberries (diced)

CRUST

    2 (9 oz.) graham cracker crust

Step 1: Drain juice from pineapples and transfer to a large mixing bowl and add the peaches and strawberry. Add lemon juice and mix. Set aside.

Step 2: In a separate mixing bowl, mix cool whip and condense milk together. Pour cool whip mixture into fruit bowl and mix well. Transfer fruit and cool whip mixture to pie crusts. Place in refrigerator overnight for firmness. Slice up and enjoy. Make 6 to 8 servings.

Cooking Advisory Tip: This recipe can be made into parfaits, if you decide to go camping in the jungle.

GROWN FOLKS COOKIES AND CREAM

If you like cookies and cream, than you will love my version of "Grown Folks Cookies and Cream." This homemade ice cream will allow you to create grown folks' memories for as long as you are stocked up with these ingredients. Forget you are lactose intolerant, it does not matter anymore. By the time you have a couple scopes of this ice cream, you won't remember why you were so intolerable in the first place.

INGREDIENTS

14 chocolate sandwich cookies
1 ½ cup light cream
3 tbsps. Coconut rum
4 tbsps. Kahlua

In a blender, add the cookies, cream, rum, and Kahlua. Puree until smooth and scoop into a small bowl. Place in the freezer overnight or 5 hours for firmness. Serve solo or with whip cream. Make 4 to 6 servings.

Cooking Advisory Tip: If you want your children to enjoy some this ice cream, remove the liquor from this recipe–we don't want them getting grown too fast!

PROTECTED CHOCOLATE BARS

A couple of years ago, there was a rumor going around, there was going to be a potential chocolate shortage. I was hoping there was no validity to this rumor. Just the thought of a chocolate shortage, is a bit unsettling. Who knows what people will do to get their chocolate fix on. There could be a chocolate pandemic that can cause:

* Truck drivers of prominent candy companies to be kidnapped by "manless" women;
* Pastry chefs to confess their chocolate garnish was really a cover-up for their bad tasting chocolate desserts; and
* The end of a 20 year dance career of a "bill collector"–whose stage name is "Hot Chocolate (HC)!"

These are some of the few "dramatic situations" that could occur, if there's a chocolate shortage. If you want to be prepared for a possible chocolate shortage, I suggest that you get started with this recipe to protect your chocolate from being stolen.

INGREDIENTS

2 cups graham crackers (finely grated)
1 cup oats (finely grated)
1 cup coconut flakes (toasted)
10 tbsps. unsalted butter (melted)
Nonstick spray

CHOCOLATE SAUCE

    2 tbsps. margarine
    1 cup semi-sweet chocolate morsels
    1 tbsp. fluff
    3 ½ cups water

Preheat oven to 350° degrees.

Step 1: In a medium non-stick skillet, toast coconut flakes for approximately 2 minutes and set aside.

Step 2: In a Food Processor, pulse graham crackers and oats until finely grated. Transfer to a large mixing bowl. Mix graham crackers, oats, and toasted coconut flakes together. Add melted butter and mix until butter is incorporated. Spray 9X13 casserole dish with nonstick spray. Pour mixture into dish and pack down mixture with measuring cup until evenly spread. Bake in oven for 12 minutes. Remove from oven and cool for 1 hour. Set aside.

Step 3: For the sauce, place a sauce pan on stovetop and add water. Place a mixing bowl over the boiling water and add margarine and chocolate morsels. Stir until morsels have completely melted. Fold in fluff and remove pan from stovetop. Spread the entire mixture over HALF of the prepared graham oats crust. Using a sharp knife, cut the uncovered HALF of the graham crust in the middle, and place it over the chocolate covered graham oats. Place casserole dish back in refrigerator to firm. Cut bars and enjoy. Make 6 to 8 serving.

Cooking Advisory Tip: You might want to stock up on your favorite chocolate candy bars, just in case, this rumor is really true.

CHAPTER 9

Happy and Happier Drinks: Beverages that will allow one to slowly confess all of their hidden indiscretions.

• • •

Happy/Unhappy Lemonade

Down in the south, there is a lot of lemonade being consumed by some very happy people. For some reason, this happiness has become contagious whenever there's a pitcher of it "stirred" up. This might explain why there is a lot of rocking on the porch. Once I realized why everybody was so happy, I decided to make me a batch up–to see what was really bringing out this happiness in people. So, I set out to test this recipe on my Latino neighbor who was always complaining about how her boss was mistreating her. Within 30 minutes of sipping, there was no more mention of her ruthless boss. I couldn't believe it, I had concocted a batch of lemonade that would make someone forget the reason they were unhappy. I guess that "C" average in Science was finally working in my favor.

It is my wish, that everybody will invite some happiness in their lives, while they still have their health and strength to consume it. It would be a shame, to go through life being unhappy, just because negative spirits has somewhat invited themselves into your presence. For once, put your wig on the wig head, and go get you some happiness in you. This is your time to be extra happy!

Ingredients

1 ½ cup of lemon juice
4 tbsps. Rum
4 tbsps. Tequila
2 quarter sizes fresh ginger (sliced and peeled)
1 cup raw sugar
3 cups water

Step 1: In a kettle, add 3 cups of water and ginger. Bring to a boil and remove from stovetop when the kettle "hollas" back at you. Allow ginger water to completely cool.

Step 2: In the pitcher, add lemon juice, sugar, Rum, and Tequila. Stir until all ingredients are blended. Pour ginger water along with the whole ginger into the lemonade. Chill lemonade in refrigerator overnight or serve immediately with crush ice–if you can't wait to be happy.

Mixing Advisory Tip #1: If you are drinking "Happy Lemonade," please drink in the comforts of your home and not on the road. I don't want you to go from being happy, to being locked the hell up!

UNHAPPY LEMONADE

- 1 ½ cup of lemon juice
- 2 quarter sizes fresh ginger (sliced and peeled)
- 2 tbsps. agave nectar
- 3 cups water

Step 1: Follow steps of "Happy Lemonade" recipe without the Rum and Tequila ingredients.

Mixing Advisory Tip #2: For the "Unhappy Lemonaders (UL)," this recipe was not written specifically for persons who were unhappy. This lemonade is for persons who were trying to limit their sugar intake because they were already "sweet" enough.

SANGRIA CONFESSIONS

Have you been running from grocery store to grocery store, trying to find a readymade bottle of Sangria for the girls "Exhale" party? Stop running, there's no need to stalk that fine looking Store Manager any longer. Save your energy by making up a jug yourself. It's guaranteed to make your guest laugh, shout, and confess their hidden secrets–all in one sitting. Maybe after a couple of rounds of this Sangria, you might finally have closure on which one of your girlfriends convinced your boyfriend to break off your engagement.

GINGER SYRUP WATER

2 cloves fresh ginger
2 ½ cups water
1 cup raw sugar

Step 1: In a kettle, add water, ginger, and sugar. Bring to a boil and remove from stovetop when kettle "hollas" back at you. Strain ginger syrup water into a pitcher and refrigerator overnight.

FRUIT MIXTURE

1 orange (sliced w/peels)
1 apple (sliced w/peels)
1 peach (sliced w/peels)
½ cup of orange juice
1 (1 oz.) bottle of Whisky or Tequila
2 bottles of Pinot Gorgio Wine

Step 2: Pour ginger syrup water, orange juice, wine, and whisky or tequila into the pitcher. Stir in slice orange, apple, and peach. Mix well and serve up for some juicy confessions.

Mixing Advisory Tip: Make sure you "alert" your guests of the potency of this Sangria. As always, be a good host and don't allow anyone behind the wheel while they are buzzed up or too overwhelmed with laughter.

Blackberry, Strawberry, Basil & Shine

If you were African American residing in the rural south in the '60s, you were probably hanging out at the local Shot House (SH) for the comradery and good times. For most patrons at the SH, it was the one place you could be yourself and be stress free from a difficult work week. From the perspective of the self-righteous folks within the community, you were considered to be a "sinner" if you were spotted at the SH. Of course that was not the case of my father, he just somehow just happened to be in close proximity when folks were drinking "flaming" water, frying up food, and playing cards.

Whenever I rode with my father to transport kin folks and his friends to the SH, it was like taking a field trip to a monumental landmark. I enjoyed tagging along to the SH because the patrons would give me pickle pig feet, canned sardines, potted meat, penny candy, and pocket change–to ensure I would not "snitch" on my father or them. Although those "hush snacks" were everything a greedy eating little girl wished for, there was a little guilt from indulging in those delicious treats. See, I was also being rewarded homecooked meals at the local diner, for being my mother's "Kiddy Informant (KI)." I guess in the spy world, I would have been considered a "Double Agent" with extra benefits.

As I got older, I began to realize the SH was more than a hangout spot for the so called sinners. It was a place where folks could:

* Help themselves to free food when money was too scarce from a low paying job;
* Utilize their pocket change in a low funded card game, in hopes of winning enough money to pay an overdue bill; and

* Pay an underutilized kid to bring their Uncles and Aunts a glass of "flaming" water–so they could one day be knowledgeable about managing their own restaurant establishment.

The SH was more than a place to obtain a shot of liquor, it was our Safe Haven. Although my father and SH generation has passed on, the memories of how they looked out for each other, with little resources, will always bring me humility. Let's raise our jars and jugs, to the Shot House!

INGREDIENTS

1(6 oz.) container blackberries
1 cup strawberries
2 tbsps. fresh basil
1 cup homemade lime juice (3 freshly squeeze limes w/ 3 tbsp. of Agave Nectar)
2 tbsps. blackberry moonshine
½ cup ice

In a mason jar, muddle basil, blackberries, and strawberries. Add lime juice and moonshine. Top with a lid and shake mixture up. Remove lid and strain berries and basil to extract the liquids into a drinking glass. Add ice and enjoy.

Cooking Advisory Tip: The moonshine for this recipe can be purchased at your local liquor store. I wanted to make sure you knew this critical information–before you drove down an isolated dirt road in search of an "Unemployed Moonshiner (UM)."

"Dreamy" Dreamsicle

When we dream, we sometimes have difficulties analyzing what a dream is trying to reveal to us. Some dreams might be trying to tell you, it's time to film your very own "bootleg" reality show–to expose your family indiscretions. You never know what a dream is trying to tell you, when consuming hard liquor. For instance, if you had a dream that you:

* Were married to pig farmer on a beautiful 40 acre ranch with peace and tranquility–this means you and the pigs will be removed from civilization;
* Became a vegetarian and you were being chased by bull with "Corn on the Cob" horns–this might be an indication you need to eat some meat;
* Are indulging in caviar and married to a rich football player–this could mean you will become a conniving "Gold Digger"; and
* Were surrounded by wolves in a secluded area of the woods, and they don't eat you–this could mean you have lots of enemies in your office, but they will not harm you because they know you are having "dramatic episodes" with the supervisor.

These are just a few scenarios that will hopefully assist you with analyzing your dreams. In the meantime, while you are trying to figure out your dreams, I do hope that you fulfill my dreams, of having lots of laughter after making this "dreamy" drink. This is my dream–please don't try to analyze it.

INGREDIENTS

1 quart orange sherbet
½ cup peach vodka (reserve ¼ cup)
1 (8 oz.) container cool whip
1 jar maraschino cherries (diced)

Step 1: Once you open the jar of maraschino cherries, drain the juice in a cup. Mix juice with ½ cup of vodka and set aside.

Step 2: Dump cherries into a small mixing bowl and ¼ cup of re-serve vodka. Soak cherries in vodka for 1 hour and set aside.

Step 3: In a mixing bowl, pour the vodka cherry juice into the sher-bet and mix. This mixture will become the vodka ice cream.

Step 4: In a desert glasses, layer the following: 1) Vodka ice cream; 2) cool whip; and 3) vodka cherries. Repeat steps and garnish top layer with whip cream. Place dreamsicle in freezer for 15 minutes to keep chilled. Take out freezer 10 minutes prior to serving guest. Hand out and enjoy your dreams. Make 2 to 4 servings.

Cooking Advisory Tip: If want the children to enjoy this drink, remove the alcohol and follow the recipe in the order given.

CHAPTER 10

Get in Touch with the Earth: Produce recipes for persons who are deeply in touch with the earth.

• • •

Spiral Zucchini w/ Meat Sauce

For the people who are trying to pull back from the table because you have been hammering down on too much pasta, this recipe should keep your stomach company until you have decided to end your love affair with pasta. Be mindful, this might be a difficult break-up. Try not to reminisce too much on your roller coaster relationship of raised blood glucose levels. It will only delay the time you will need, to pick up that "spiral cutter," and get to working on shredding that zucchini! Let's start today, by mending your relationship with your first love–the vegetable.

Ingredients

4 medium size zucchinis
½ tsp. salt (optional)
½ tsp. black pepper
1 tbsp. oil

Sauce

1 pound ground chicken
2 cups grape tomatoes
1 cup onions
3 garlic cloves
5 basil sprigs (fresh)
¼ tsp. salt (optional)
¼ tsp. black pepper
2 tbsps. vegetable oil (reserve 1 tbsp. for roasting)

Preheat oven at 350° degrees.

Baked Zucchinis: On a sheet pan, drizzle oil. Using the spiral cutter, shred zucchini directly on oiled sheet pan. Sprinkle zucchini with salt and pepper. Toss with your hands for even distribution and place in oven for 15 minutes.

Meat Sauce: On the stovetop, preheat oil in a non-stick skillet. Add onions, garlic, salt, and pepper, sauté for 5 minutes or until translucent. Add ground chicken and fully cook. Add tomatoes and basil, cook for an additional 25 minutes or until sauce has thicken. Remove from stovetop and serve over zucchini. Make 4 to 6 servings.

Cooking Advisory Tip: This is a good recipe if you are trying to incorporate less carbohydrates and more vegetables and protein into your meals.

CARROT RAISIN PINEAPPLE CASSEROLE

As a child, did your parent(s) ever say, "Don't play with your vegetables!" If so, this was probably not the best advice for a child who was trying to express to their parent(s) the food was horrible. Of course the child did not want to hurt their parents' feelings, but at the same time, they did not want to jeopardize their future job prospects of being a Publicist for a "ratchet" politician either. So they do what any precious little child would do, they suffered with eating the worst tasting food–until they left home for good.

A child should be encouraged to examine their vegetables, but in a different way. For instance, as a parent, you can have the child pretend they are a "Food Critic (FC)" who analyzes homecooked meals for taste and originality. A scoring system can be establish to rate the meals being served in your house. Their likes and dislikes of your food, will determine if your child should cook all future meals in your household, or be the one to go grocery shopping for food items. However this matter is resolved in your house, I wish you all the best. Remember, I'm here to give you a resolution recipe, not to find a solution to an unexplainable demand.

INGREDIENTS

3 cups carrots (puree)
1 cup crushed pineapple (reserve ½ cup of pineapple juice)
½ cup coconut (soak w/ extract)
½ cup raisins
1 tsp. cinnamon
¼ tsp. nutmeg

1 tsp. coconut extract
3 egg whites (1 egg yolk)
½ cup milk

Preheat oven 360° degrees.

Step 1: In a mixing bowl, mix together carrots, pineapple, coconut, raisins, cinnamon, and nutmeg. Set aside.

Step 2: In a small mixing bowl, mix egg whites, egg yolks, milk, extract, and pineapple juice together. Pour custard over carrot mixture. Place in oven and bake covered for 35 minutes, with the last 15 minutes uncovered. Remove from oven to cool and garnish with whip cream. Make 4 servings.

Cooking Advisory Tip: This is a family friendly recipe that should be right tasty if it's executed correctly. If for some reason this recipe becomes tasteless after prepared, please refrain from giving it to your child. Lord knows, children don't lie.

Lunch Packer Apple Walnut Salad

This recipe is for the "Lunch Packer (LP)" who cries endlessly for not being able to decide, what to pack for their little offspring's lunch. Don't sweat it, I somewhat feel your stress. I wouldn't say, "I know your stress," if I did, that would make me a very dishonest and shady person. Let's just say, "I'm sympathetic to your problem."

It's a job in itself trying to plan lunch for demanding little offspring. Its times like this, you probably wish you could adopt a starving homeless dog without a home—it's still not too late to fill out the adoption papers at the local animal shelter. Anyway, it's unfortunate you don't have any control in your house. Don't fret, maybe I can relieve your headache with a stress free recipe. It might not resolve all of your lunch problems, but at least it will keep the little offspring's mouth occupied until your next lunch packing day–best of luck.

Ingredient

2 macintosh or granny smith apples (diced)
½ cup of vanilla yogurt
1 ½ cup black walnuts (favorite nut or mini chocolate chips)
1 tsp. cinnamon
1 cup raisin
1 tsp. lemon juice

In a mixing bowl, mix apples and lemon juice; marinate for 5 minutes. Fold in cinnamon, raisins, and yogurt; mix well. Top with walnuts and refrigerator overnight. Make 2 servings.

Cooking Advisory Tip: If you are a LP who's tired of packing lunch bags for the little offspring, just tell them, you will be going back to school to become a Nutritionist–and they need to learn how to pack your lunch!

CANTALOUPE GINGER BASIL GRATIN

Living on a farm, it was normal for me to see my father utilizing the tractor or mule, in preparation for crop season. He was always working, and working us around the clock to keep the farm operating. I recall one particular summer, my father decided to plant cantaloupes in an underutilized field. As the cantaloupes would start to grow, my father would walk pass every day to observe its progress. By the time late summer had arrived, those cantaloupes had blossomed into a beautiful indulgence.

The day of my 10th birthday, my father had me walk with him to the field where the cantaloupes were residing. Being a tough man, who worked so hard to hide his comedic side, he pointed his finger to the field and said, "Happy Birthday, these are for you." What a surprise, I couldn't believe it–all those cantaloupes were for me! I was the happiest kid who ever lived on an isolated dark road. I had enough cantaloupes for my mother, my siblings, the neighbors, the stray dogs, the cows, the pigs, the mule, the deer, raccoons, rabbits, and pretty much everybody in the county. It sure felt good to be able to give everybody some of my birthday present.

Today, whenever I go to the produce aisle of a grocery store, and see cantaloupes, it brings back heartfelt memories of my 10th birthday. The memories of my father working in the field to produce a cantaloupe garden for me, was confirmation that my father loved me unconditionally. He showed me how love can be expressed in different ways. If there was a life lesson for this happy memory, it would have to be, "We should all show gratitude for the produce that comes from the earth, and the manual labor that initiated the process, for the produce to come up from the earth."

INGREDIENTS

2 cantaloupes (remove seeds)
1 tbsp. lime juice
1 tsp. fresh ginger (grated)
1 ½ tbsp. fresh basil

Step 1: Place cantaloupe, ginger, basil, and lime juice into blender. Puree until it becomes a liquidy.

Step 2: Pour mixture into a 9X13 casserole glass dish and place in freezer. After 2 hours in the freezer, run a fork through the cantaloupe mixture. Wait another hour and repeat process. When ready to eat, scoop up and enjoy a summer desert in memory of my father. Make 8 servings.

Note: Reserve 1 cup of liquid from the puree, to pour over gratin, after it's removed from the freezer–for a "slushy" drink.

Cooking Advisory Tip: This would be a great dessert for the kids on a hot summer day. Once you make this gratin, they will appreciate that you took the time to transform a produce into a heartfelt moment.

OUT OF WORK CAULIFLOWER & MUSHROOM NOODLES

There's not a person living that has not been fired or ran off from a job. Sometimes it does not matter how you were fired, the question is, "Did you know you were fired?" What do I mean by this statement, let me explain.

It was the summer of 1985 and I wanted to earn some extra money to finance my new life in Washington, D.C. In order to achieve this goal, I applied for a job at the local shoe factory to confirm to my parents–that my brother really did have a job. After a couple of weeks had passed, I received a call from the Plant Manager (PM), that I was hired.

Day 1: After eating another free meal from our parents, my brother and I carpooled to work like normal working class people. Once we arrived at the factory, my brother clocked in for his shift and introduced me to the PM. As the PM proceeded to give me a tour of my work area, he introduced me to the machine I would be working on. He told me, "I would be gluing the back stem of shoes and that I had to produce two racks of shoes to meet the daily quota," which consist of 40 shoes a day. Well, I knew right then, there was going to be a problem. There was no way I would be able to complete this big task and have enough time to eat my mother's delicious shopping bag lunch. I guess I had to make it work, if I wanted to become a City girl.

Within an hour of working the shoe machine, the hot glue burned me, my finger was smashed, and the machine pinched my stomach from being too close and personal. All that pain and suffering was from one trouble making shoe. It was so upset, I just cried.

Eventually, my brother was paged over the loud speaker to come over to shut me up, so the manager would not get in trouble for conspiring with that machine to hurt me. Once my brother talked to me, I got myself together, and attempted to meet the daily quota for that lopsided shoe.

Day 2: The next day, the nagging rooster was yelling for me to get up for work. When I arrived at work, the PM was waiting patiently for me at the "enemy" machine. I believed he said, "Good morning, I'm sorry, but things are not working out." I responded okay, and worked the rest of my 7 ¾ hour shift by greeting the workers entering the factory. Being a people-oriented type person, the "factory greeter" job was more suited for me than the shoe making job. I couldn't believe it, things were finally beginning to look up for me.

Day 3: It was a normal work day for me, my mother had packed my shopping bag lunch, and I was patiently waiting for my brother to chauffeur me to work. When my brother came to the car, he had a strange look on his face. I didn't know if he was upset that Mother had given me a shopping bag lunch, or if he had another nightmare of trying to saddle up our "sleepy" mule. Eventually, he released the words from his mouth to justify the strange look on his face.

Big Brother
"Where are you going?"

Baby Girl
"I'm going to work."

Big Brother
Didn't the manager say, "Things were not working out?"

Baby Girl
"Yeah!"

Big Brother
"I believe that meant you were fired."

Baby Girl
"I thought he meant things were not working out on yesterday, and maybe it would work out better today. I didn't know I was fired!"

Big Brother
"That's what he meant."

Baby Girl
"He should have said I was fired instead of beating around the brush!"
(Removed myself from the car, and went into the house to give my father back his lunch.)

Being fired on my first job was a devastating time for me. If there was a life lesson to take away from that first job experience, it would have to be, "Employers should properly train their managers to say the word "fired" when terminating an employee, instead of allowing them to rehearse their break-up talks at the workplace!"

Ingredients

    1 whole cauliflower floret (chop close to floret)
    1 (8oz.) pkg. baby bella mushroom
    2 cups yolk free homestyle ribbon noodles

2 tbsps. taco seasoning (reserve tbsp. at end to taste)
2 cups water
¼ tsp. black pepper
2 garlic cloves
4 tbsps. unsalted butter
3 tbsps. canola oil
Salt to taste

Step 1: In a sauce pan, bring water to boil. Add noodles and cook according to package directions. Drain the noodles and reserve 2 tbsp. of water for the vegetables.

Step 2: Preheat a nonstick pan, add oil and butter. Toss in cauliflower, mushroom, reserve water, and garlic; sauté vegetables until translucent. With a potato masher, mash cauliflower and add taco seasoning, black pepper, and salt to taste.

Step 3: Fold noodles into vegetables and plate up. Make 4 to 6 servings.

Cooking Advisory Tip: This is a meal for persons who have a "gut" feeling they will be fired by the "Close of Business (COB)." Once you receive this confirmation, try not to get all upset. Look at it this way, being fired from a job, is just life way of saying, "You need to hurry up and find your destiny–before you are evicted by another landlord!"

Hockless Collards

Growing up on a farm, there was plenty of fresh produce. When it came time to harvesting our fall garden, there were collard greens, turnip greens, and curly kale. From that greenery, the curly kale and turnip greens were the most eaten in our household. That's not to say we did not enjoy collards–it was one of those situations whereas, "If there were no demands to cook it, there were no demands to eat it."

When my mother did prepare collards greens, I recall her using a ham hock. The aftermath, the collards were well-seasoned and delicious. From this indulgence, I realize, almost any meat that was smoked and salty, could pretty much season a pot of collards. These two components was the key to making collards taste delicious and making you dizzy.

The lesson from this storyline is not to suggest a ham hock is not valued, believe me, they are. I'm not trying to make anyone feel guilt. All I'm saying is, "If you chose not use a ham hock in your next pot of collards, you will not be a "hockless" person."

Ingredients

2 pounds of collards
6 smoke turkey necks or 1 turkey drumstick
1 tsp. hot pepper flakes (optional)
1 tbsp. salt
1 tbsp. of sugar
24 cups of water (reserve 12 cups)

Cleaning: Fill kitchen sink up with water and salt. Remove stem from greens and chop greens into thin ribbons. Submerge greens into water, allow them sit for 15 minutes or until dirt and grit is at the bottom of water.

In a large pot, add water and bring to a boil. Transfer collards from the sink to pot and boil for approximately 40 minutes to remove all particles. Drain collards into a colander and rinse with cold water to stop the cooking process.

Cooking: In the same pot, rinse it out and wipe out with a paper towel. Add reserve cups of water and bring to a boil. Add turkey parts and cook for 45 minutes to season the water. Transport collards to the pot, and add salt, sugar, and pepper flakes. Reduce heat, and cook for approximately 2 ½ hours or until tender. Enjoy these well season and tender greens. Make 6 servings.

Cooking Advisory Tip: Whether you prefer ham hocks or turkey parts for cooking collard greens, it is solely your decision. I'm just here for moral support.

Rhubarb Apple Parfait

If you like rhubarb and apple, this is the dessert for you. The transformation of these produces is like two strangers finding true love, just in the nick of time. Try this parfait, and holla back if you enjoy it.

Ingredients

1 stem rhubarb
1 delicious apple
¼ tsp cinnamon
1 tbsp. raw sugar
1/8 tsp. cayenne pepper
¼ tsp orange zest
1 tsp of orange juice
¼ cup of raisins
¼ tsp fresh ginger
¼ cup of coconut flakes (toasted)
1 tbsp. butter

Step 1: In a medium non-stick pan, melt butter and sauté the ruba, apples, cinnamon, sugar, cayenne pepper, orange zest, and ginger until translucent. Add orange juice and raisins into rhubarb mixture. Cook for 12 minutes and transfer mixture to a mixing bowl and set aside.

Mascarpone Cheese/Yogurt mixture

½ cup mascarpone cheese
½ cup plain greek yogurt
1 tsp. of vanilla extract
1 tbsp. confectionary sugar

Step 2: In a mixing bowl, mix mascarpone, yogurt, extract, and sugar together. In a dessert cup, first place the rhubarb mixture and then the mascarpone cheese mixture. Repeat process until and cream mixture is on top layer. Garnish with coconut flakes and keep in refrigerator until ready to serve. Make 2 servings.

Cooking Advisory Tip: Serve the parfait to the picky eater in your house. If they approve of the taste, they will have a career as a professional "Food Columnist" for a national food magazine.

Horseradish Pea Hummus

In my world, when it comes to making hummus, you can pretty much puree any starchy vegetable for dipping. If you are a skeptic, who is reluctant to dip into some hummus, you might want to attempt to make your own, to get the deliciousness you desire. If you are ready for change, this is the hummus recipe for you.

Ingredients

1 (16 oz.) bag tiny green peas
4 tbsps. thick-n-creamy horseradish
1 garlic clove (roasted)
2 tbsps. unsalted butter
½ tsp. salt
1 cup water

Preheat oven to 350° degrees.

Step 1: Cut an entire clove of garlic across the top and add oil. Place in foil and secure tightly. Place wrapped garlic on sheet pan and bake in oven for 20 minutes. Remove garlic from oven and squeeze in a small bowl. Smash until smooth and set aside.

Step 2: In a medium saucepan, add water and butter. Bring water to a boil and add peas. Cook uncovered until all the water has been absorbed. Remove peas from stovetop and season with salt. Transfer peas to food processor, add horseradish and smash garlic. Puree until all ingredients are incorporated. Transfer to a dipping bowl and serve with your favorite meat, raw vegetable, or chip. Make 6 to 8 servings.

Cooking Advisory Tip: This is good hummus to give to a love one, who's has been a little bit under the weather. The horseradish ingredient will definitely kick them back into reality.

Don't Lay Off the Sauces

If you want to hit the sauce, without being given a sobriety test from an inquisitive police officer, these sauces and dressing are guaranteed to not give you a mug shot. Try them, and take your meats, salads, and dips to another level.

Cooking Advisory Tip: Since these recipes calls for roasting whole garlic in the oven, roast a couple of whole cloves whenever you are utilizing the oven to cook a meal. Cook it ahead time and refrigerate it. I don't want you to waste gas or electricity just for one whole garlic clove.

CHAPTER 11

Don't lay off the Sauce: Sauces that will not require you to have a sobriety test.

• • •

Peppercorn Salad Dressing

½ (16 oz.) sour cream
1 cup buttermilk
1 cup mayonnaise
2 tbsps. horseradish
1 roasted whole garlic (squeeze out 3 cloves after making a paste)
1 red bell pepper
1 tbsp. black pepper
1 ½ tsp. agave
1 ½ tsp. lime juice
1 tbsp. garlic powder
1 tbsp. onion powder
1 ½ tbsp. olive oil

In a mixing bowl, mix the sour cream, buttermilk, mayonnaise, horseradish, garlic, and bell pepper. Add lime juice, garlic powder, onion powder, black pepper, and agave. Fold in olive oil and chill overnight in refrigerator for the flavors to marry each other.

Honey Horseradish Dressing

1 egg yolk (room temperature)
2 tbsps. horseradish
2 tbsps. dijon mustard
2 tbsps. honey (agave or corn syrup is fine as well)
1 tbsp. black pepper

In a mixing bowl, mix egg yolk, horseradish, mustard, honey, and black pepper. Refrigerate for 2 hours or overnight. Use on hamburgers, chicken fingers, or as a salad dressing.

SMOKY STICKY WINGS SAUCE

2 Chipotle Peppers in Adobo Sauce
1 cup ketchup
2 tbsps. honey mustard
2 tbsps. soy sauce
1 tsp. cumin
½ tsp. smoky paprika
1½ tsp. agave
2 tbsps. lime juice

Step 1: Finely chop chipotle peppers.

Step 2: In a mixing bowl, add ketchup, mustard, soy sauce, agave, cumin, smoky paprika, and lime juice. Pour mixture into a small sauce pan and bring to a broil. Cook sauce until thicken.

Step 3: Remove saucepan from stovetop and toss your fried or baked chicken and enjoy this "smoky" flavored sauce.

Ms. Pearl's Barbecue Sauce

1 cup ketchup
1 cup apple cider vinegar
2 tbsps. Worchester sauce
½ cup brown sugar
1 tsp. onion powder
1 tsp. garlic powder
1 tbsp. cumin
¼ cup fresh ginger root
2 tbsps. sweet orange marmalade
¼ tsp. cayenne pepper

In a saucepan, add ketchup, vinegar, Worchester sauce, brown sugar, onion powder, garlic powder, cumin, ginger root, marmalade, and cayenne pepper. Bring to a boil for 10 minutes. Simmer on low heat for 15 minutes. Remove from stovetop and use sauce for basing grilled meats.

RED PEPPER BUTTERMILK MARINADE

1 cup buttermilk
1 medium red bell pepper (cut into quarters)
1 medium onion (cut into quarters)
1 whole garlic (cut tops of cloves and roast in oven)
2 tbsps. olive oil
1 tsp. salt
1 tbsp. black pepper

Preheat oven to 370° degrees.

Step 1: On a sheet pan, place bell pepper and onions. Sprinkle with salt and pepper. Cut top off garlic, add oil, and wrap with foil (roast with other vegetables). Cook vegetables for 25 minutes. Remove from oven and cool for 5 minutes.

Step 2: In a Food Processor, squeeze the garlic cloves and add vegetables. Puree and gradually pour buttermilk until veggies are well incorporated. Pour into a jar and refrigerate for a poultry or turkey marinade.

"IN LOVING MEMORY OF NEWTON"

CHAPTER 12

Newton's Corner: Rememberable canine cuisine just for Newton.

• • •

NEWTON'S CHICKEN ROLLS

This comedic cookbook would not be complete if I did not acknowledge my beloved dog, Newton. On September 1, 2000, I adopted Newton from the Prince George's County Animal Management Division (AMD) after he was picked up by Animal Control in the suburbs of Maryland. Upon his arrival at the shelter, Newton was in a bad way. He was trembling, suffering from a bad cold, and his hair was matted–he did not look like a Maltese. Once he was bathed and groomed, Newton was on his way to making a fresh start in his new home.

After a couple of weeks of occupancy, it did not take Newton anytime to realize he had hit the jackpot. From my observation, there was no indication that he was ever homeless or abused. That might have been solely because he was receiving the red carpet treatment at my house. His new found lifestyle gave him nice wearing doggy apparel, plush monogramed doggy beds, and homecooked doggy cuisine. He was living the life of a king, without the responsibilities of a kingdom.

Whenever I prepared Newton's meals, the little critter was consuming so much food, I thought he was a moving storage unit. Every time I turned around, his head was buried in his doggy bowl. I don't know if he was hungry, or if he was using some kind of "doggy sign language" as a way to get more food. He was eating better than some patrons at a five-star restaurant.

If you are curious to find out why Newton deserved to be so happy, take the time to prepare "Newton's Chicken Rolls," and allow your pooch to live like royalty.

INGREDIENTS

    2 cups chicken tenderloins (finely chopped)
    1 ¼ cup chicken stock (reserve 2 tbsp. for basing)
    2 cups white wheat flour
    3 eggs whites (reserve 1 egg yolk)

Preheat oven to 350° degrees.

Step 1: In a small sauce pan, add chicken stock and bring to a boil. Add chicken and cook for approximately 5 minutes. Pour stock into a bowl and cool. Remove chicken from pan to cool as well. Chop up chicken and set aside.

Step 2: In a mixing bowl, add flour, egg whites, yolk, and chicken stock. Mix together until it becomes a dough. Wrap dough and place in refrigerator for 15 minutes to firm. Remove dough from refrigerator and rest for 15 minutes.

Step 3: On the countertop, flour the surface and rolling pin. Place dough on countertop and roll out. With a round biscuit mold, cut out dough to roll out into 4 inch circles. Once dough is rolled, add 1 tbsp. of pot boiled chicken to the center of dough. Fold dough over chicken, and roll until the seam of dough is tucked downwards on countertop. Place chicken roll on sheet pan with parchment paper and repeat process until all the chicken rolls have been prepared.

Step 4: With a pastry brush, brush each chicken roll with some leftover chicken stock. Bake chicken rolls for 20 minutes. Remove for oven and cool before serving to your precious pooch. Makes 10 to 12 chicken rolls.

Cooking Advisory Tip: To the dog parent(s) out there, once you start to make these chicken rolls, your pooch will be expecting them on a regular basis. If you chose to stop making these chicken rolls, there will be fewer greetings from your dog when you come home from a stressful day at work–I'm just saying.

NEWTON'S LOVE PATTIES

When my father and Newton met for the first time, it was not acceptance at first sight. My father was old school, whereas, he believed dogs belong outside in the elements. I was sympathetic to my father's concerns for a short period of time. Being a Home Cook who focuses on resolution recipes to solve problems, I had to pull out all of my cooking strategies to find a diplomatic way, to change my father's unfavorable decision regarding Newton's housing arrangement.

Before my precious little Newton would be shown the other side of the door, I had to transform my father's thought process about dogs. Once I had a deep discussion to explain Newton's abandonment issues, and possible delays of homecooked meals, my father somehow saw things my way. Understand, my father was a product of the Great Depression era, whereas a homecooked meal was like a precious jewel. There was no way my father was going to jeopardize a delicious southern meal just to serve my Newton an "eviction notice." I tell you, being a Home Cook sure can have positive outcomes, if you are willing to put in the work!

Over the years, my father and Newton became best buddies. They would take car rides to the Shot House (SH) and eat late evening snacks together. They had gotten so close–my father began experimenting with braiding techniques on Newton's long locks. That act of love was more than enough confirmation, that my father had put aside his dislikes of dogs, to concentrate on what really mattered–being a grandfather to his only granddog.

Ingredients

> 1 lb. lean ground beef (95%/7% fat)
> 1 ¼ cup peas
> ½ cup fresh carrots
> 1 cup beef stock
> 1 tbsp. flour

Preheat oven to 350° degrees.

Step 1: In a small pan add beef stock and bring to boil. Add peas and carrots and cook for 5 minutes. Cool and set aside.

Step 2: In a food processor, puree peas, carrots, and flour. Once mixture has been incorporated, transfer to a mixing bowl and cool for 10 minutes.

Step 3: Once veggies are cooled, add the ground beef and mix with hands. Transfer beef mixture on parchment paper and spread out with hand. Using a heart shape cookie cutter, cut out each patty and place on sheet pan. Place in the oven and bake for 15 minutes. Remove from oven and base with more beef stock. Allow them to completely cool and serve to your pooch. Make 6 patties.

Cooking Advisory Tip: If your dog does not have long locks, you might not want to attempt to braid their hair–a pat on the head will probably suffice.

NEWT'S BACON BISCUITS

As a dog parent, you must always have a batch of homemade treats for your pooch for spoiling purposes. If your dog has been loyal to you, when everyone has turned their backs on you, they deserve to be treated like a king or queen. Who cares about the negative comments from your family and friends–they are probably wishing that someone was preparing a homemade treat for them. Ignore them, and take special care of your four-legged pooch–I rest these dog biscuits on that!

INGREDIENTS

2 cups flour
½ cup egg whites
½ cup bacon bits
½ cup chicken stock

Preheat oven to 350° degrees.

Step 1: In a mixing bowl, mix flour and egg whites with hands. Fold in bacon bits into the dough. Gradually add chicken stock. When dough is pliable; transfer dough to a floured countertop. Roll dough with a rolling pin until it has expanded.

Step 2: Using a doggie bone cookie cutter, cut out the bones until all dough is utilized. Once all bones are cut out, place on a sheet pan with parchment paper. Base each bone with chicken stock. Place in oven, and bake for 20 minutes. Remove from oven and base with chicken stock for the final time. Cool and serve your pooch a home-made treat. Make 4 to 6 biscuits.

Cooking Advisory Tip: If you know your neighbor has not been spoiling their pooch, just box up some of these treats. Once they are all packaged up, make sure you place a note inside the package that says, "Your dog has been looking sad lately, I assume he or she has not been getting any attention, here's some homemade treats that will allow your dog to smile again, and hopefully come back over to my house."

NEWTON'S ULTIMATE FEAST

During the holiday time, the anticipation of a delicious homecook meal is the driving force for most family gatherings. Unfortunately, for the family dog, this is not the case. They are overlooked when it comes to a homecook meal that is exclusively for them. Due to this fact, they are unable to verbally express their true feelings, so they howl in silence. Of course they want to say to their family, "I'm tired of having an upset stomach from table scraps," but they don't want to come off as being ungrateful. Believe me, your dog is trying to express an emotion to you–but you are refusing to pay them any attention.

If your dog has a furious look on their face and is refusing to eat store bought dog food, this is an indication they are suffering from Canine Holiday Exclusion (CHE) syndrome. This syndrome occurs when family dogs are excluded from holiday feast preparations. For years, this syndrome had gone undetected until a Country Lady discovered there was no barking from country dogs, living in isolated rural areas, during the holidays. Fortunately, these country dogs were cured of this syndrome–when their families finally decided to adhere to their extreme ransom demands!

In short, if you do not want your dog to experience CHE, than do something about it. Fix them up a batch of "Newton's Ultimate Feast." It will not only make your dog happy again, it will ensure your dog will continue to bark at potential burglars.

INGREDIENTS

2 cups carrots (diced)
3 cups frozen peas
4 chicken breasts (diced)

1 cup real bacon bits
1 cup chicken stock
½ cup brown rice (cook according box instructions)

Step 1: In a large sauce pan, add chicken stock and bring to boil. Add carrots and peas and cook for 15 minutes. Add chicken, the last 5 minutes of cooking time. Remove saucepan from stovetop and transfer mixture into a bowl to cool. Fold in bacon bits into mixture and set aside.

Step 2: Cook rice according to box instructions and incorporate into the feast mixture. Serve up to your pooch. Make 4 servings.

Cooking Advisory Tip: For the holidays, do a good deed, double this recipe and give a batch to the sheltered dogs in your community. They will be overjoyed that someone was kind enough to think about them.

Made in the USA
Coppell, TX
15 June 2022

78871642R00134